Contents

A Story Worth Sharing

Kelly A. Fryer, Editor

A Story Worth Sharing

ENGAGING EVANGELISM

Augsburg Fortress

Minneapolis

A STORY WORTH SHARING
Engaging Evangelism

Developed in cooperation with the Evangelical Lutheran Church in America Division for Congregational Ministries, Robert Wallace and Brent W. Dahlseng, project managers.

Augsburg Fortress editors: Laurie J. Hanson, Ivy M. Palmer, and James Satter
Interior text design: Ivy M. Palmer and James Satter
Cover design: Alisha Olson
Cover and interior illustrations: Artville
Back cover photo: Pam Schultz

ISBN 0-8066-5005-2

09   08   07   06   05   04   1   2   3   4   5   6

Will We Be Who We Say We Are?

Kelly A. Fryer

Have you ever seen a sign that you're pretty sure didn't mean what it said? How about this one, which was posted in a hospital lobby: "For anyone who has children and doesn't know it, there is a day care center on the first floor." Or this one, posted outside a second-hand store: "We exchange anything—bicycles, washing machines, etc. Why not bring your wife along and get a wonderful bargain?" One of my favorite examples of a sign that probably didn't really mean what it said was spotted on the front window of a dry cleaner's shop. It boldly invited: "We hope you'll drop your pants here."

Well, most of our congregations have a sign somewhere, too. Usually it is in a very visible location. It sits out on the lawn, close to the curb, where every passerby can see it. Or it hangs right on the building. And this is what our signs say: "Evangelical Lutheran Church in America." But, for some reason, the fact that our signs don't always mean what they say doesn't seem all that funny.

Now, it isn't the "in America" part we have trouble with. And it isn't really the "Lutheran" part, although it could be argued that we have some work to do in figuring out exactly what we mean by that. Most of us don't have trouble with the "Church" part, either. But "Evangelical" . . . who are we kidding?

In the August 2003 issue of *The Lutheran* magazine, the cover story asked a startling question: "Do We HATE Evangelism?" And it offered some compelling evidence that we, in fact, do. At the very least, evangelism and evangelizing are not activities that Lutherans have generally been too excited about. The idea of sharing our faith with fellow church members scares the daylights out of a lot of us. And we can't even imagine introducing Jesus to somebody who hasn't met him before. We are (so the argument goes) too shy. Too reserved. Too easily embarrassed. Too uncertain. Too culturally conditioned to keep our faith private. For whatever reason, the average ELCA member says that they would just rather not be involved in evangelism. When we were asked what our response would be if we were asked to visit somebody we know in order to share the gospel, a little more than 20 percent of ELCA members said we would do it reluctantly; 33 percent said we're not sure whether we'd do it or not; and almost 40 percent of us said we would just flat out refuse! (See "An Evaluation of the 1991 Evangelism Strategy" by Kenneth W. Inskeep, Evangelical Lutheran Church in America, October 3, 2000. For an in-depth look at these and other numbers, and the issues behind them, visit the ELCA Web site at www.elca.org.)

If we are really going to mean what we say on our signs, then this has to change.

No Point in Taking a Guilt Trip

But things won't change because we have been "guilted" into it. And they won't change because we have been scared into it, either, by the realization that if we don't do something our church will die.

Fear or guilt might make us pick up a book (like this one!) or attend a workshop (on pick a topic, any topic, like "creating a hospitable climate in your congregation" or "reaching out to families with young children" or "communication strategies for outreach," etc., etc., etc.). Guilt or fear might even lead us to implement some of what we have learned.

And, for a while, there might even be some good things that happen in our congregations because of it. After all, people out there really are hungry for the good news and, if we did anything at all to share it with them, chances are good they would respond.

But the new energy and growth that our congregations would experience because of our guilt-ridden or fear-induced efforts would, sooner or later, fizzle out and die. We would get tired of working so hard. We would get frustrated because the job seemed so never-ending. We would, maybe, find ourselves getting mad because all of the new people our efforts brought in have started sitting in our seats . . . and at the council table . . . and changing everything around. When all was said and done, we might discover that our congregations had ended up in even worse shape than they started in! (This is, in fact, what happened in ELCA congregations across the country during the 1990s. Check out reports from the Department for Research and Evaluation on the ELCA Web site for the whole story.)

No, if we are really going to be who we say we are—an evangelical church—it will not happen because we have been shoved into evangelizing by guilt or fear. On the contrary, we will become an evangelical people only when we have been caught up in love.

> **Evangelical people have been caught up in love . . . for the Lord our God.**

Loving the Church Is Not Enough

We are not talking here, however, about the love we have for our churches. Not that there is anything wrong with loving your church. Most of us do. We love knowing that it is there for us when we need it. We love feeling like we know the ropes, we can find the coffee pot on Sunday morning (some of us even know how to make the coffee!), and some of the prayers are so familiar we can say them with our eyes closed. We love this. We love the way our church feels like home.

No, there is nothing at all wrong with loving the church . . . unless, of course, we love it more than we love the other two things Jesus told us to love most of all. "Hear this!" Jesus said. "You shall love the Lord your God with all your heart, and with all your soul, and with all your mind, and with all your strength." He took a breath and then concluded, "You shall love your neighbor as yourself" (Mark 12:30-31).

Evangelical people have been, first of all, caught up in love . . . for the Lord our God. We know that there is nothing we could have ever done to deserve the gift we have been given. Through Jesus, God has saved us by calling us out of our old lives, out of darkness and despair and death, and into a new life of freedom and purpose and hope. Knowing exactly who and what we are, Jesus looks at us with love in his eyes anyway and says, "Come, follow me." And, so, we go. We go because we know that our lives will finally be all that they are meant to be only when we answer this call. We follow him into a new life of service and sacrifice; we willingly give ourselves away. And we know that this is what it really means to be saved by grace through faith. Our salvation is a call! And, as we answer it, our very lives become a testimony to the free gift of God's amazing grace and the mighty power of God's Spirit at work within us. We find ourselves caught up in love for the Lord and wanting, more than anything, to be a part of what God is doing in the world.

> *This is why evangelical people are, secondly, caught up in love . . . for their neighbors.*

This is why evangelical people are, secondly, caught up in love . . . for their neighbors. They know that God's heart aches wherever there are people who have not heard the call and do not know the joy that comes from being loved by the One who made them. Martin Luther even went so far as to say, "a Christian lives not in himself, but in Christ and in his neighbor. Otherwise he is not a Christian" (*On Christian Liberty* [also called *Freedom of a Christian*], Minneapolis: Fortress Press, 2003, p. 62). And, if you remember the parable of the good Samaritan, Jesus was pretty clear that a "neighbor" is not necessarily the guy who lives next door or the nice couple down the street. I am a neighbor to everyone who is in need. (Check it out for yourself in Luke 10:25-37.) And the world is full of people like that.

Maggie was one of them. She hadn't been to church in 30 years, not since the day she and her newly wed husband ran through the shower of rice on the front steps of the building. She had never even bothered to have her children baptized. One day, after a series of tragic incidents that left her spirit shattered, Maggie got a flyer in the mail from a new church in town. On most any other day, she would have thrown it in the garbage. But this day was different. She went to worship that weekend and has been back every single week ever since. Now, you can't get Maggie to stop talking about the difference this experience has made in her life. She spends herself in service, giving away her talents and her time and her money to make a difference in the congregation and in her community. She has invited every friend and family member she knows to church. She cried the day her daughter and four grandchildren were baptized. She talks about God at work. And she has discovered, to her surprise, that almost all of the people she works with every day have a church home. They talk with her, now, about the sermon they heard last weekend and the Bible study they're in and the outdoor barbeque their church is having this summer. And Maggie can't help wondering why they didn't share this stuff with her before. You know, when her world was falling apart, when she really needed it.

Evangelical people love the Lord with all their hearts and minds; and they love people like Maggie. They love God and they love their neighbors even more than they love their church.

And that is saying a lot.

This Is Where It All Begins

We will not become the evangelical people we say we are just by implementing a few new programs at church. The programs are important, to be sure. There are some techniques that work—like sending well-designed flyers inviting people like Maggie to well-planned events. We ought to know how to do this stuff. We ought to be sharing our best practices with one another and searching the world over for even better ones. But evangelism programs and outreach techniques and marketing strategies are definitely not the place to start. That is why, perhaps a little surprisingly, the Evangelism Strategy approved by the ELCA church-wide assembly in 2003 doesn't begin there. Rather, that strategy calls this church to four missional tasks:

1. Praying
2. Forming evangelical leaders
3. Raising up disciples
4. Renewing congregations and planting the church

This book is written to help our church do exactly those four things.

Part One establishes a theological and biblical foundation for thinking about evangelism. Here we address the *Why* questions and ground ourselves in what God is doing. In chapter 1, we meet the God who is madly in love with us. This God is busy saving the world, calling us out of an old life and into a new one, and inviting us, as we see in chapter 2, to be a part of it all. We explore what it means to be a member of the priesthood of all believers with a call to evangelical leadership in our church and in the world. In chapter 3, we rediscover that becoming an evangelical person begins with worship, prayer, Bible study, and the spiritual disciplines; it begins, in other words, when we meet Jesus, hear his call to discipleship, and grow in faith and understanding. Chapter 4 reminds us that evangelism is not a solo activity; it springs out of the life we share together, as members of constantly reformed and renewing congregations. And then, in chapter 5, we explore what it means to say that we serve a God who comes down, right into the middle of our lives and our communities, to make all things new. We see how taking context seriously is imperative if we are really serious about planting and growing the church today.

Part Two addresses some of the biggest *How* questions. Here we get practical about how to share the story as individuals and as congregations. Chapter 6 starts off by helping us think through what it would look like for God's mission and our evangelical identity to really shape our lives together, as God's people called and gathered together in congregations. Chapter 7 gives us a clear picture of the task of transformational leadership, the kind of leadership that will be necessary for us to become the evangelical people we say we are. Chapters 8 and 9 offer some very practical guidance for becoming people—and congregations—who love to share the faith story and invite others to meet the One who loves them. Chapters 10, 11, and 12 challenge us to consider how we must let our particular geographical, cultural, and social contexts shape our evangelical witness. The conclusion wraps things up by inviting us to consider what all of this means for those of us who belong to a church that calls itself Evangelical.

It has been my job to help provide a consistent tone and theological framework for this book. But this has truly been a team effort. The writers of these chapters—and all those who have contributed to this effort—have come together from across our church, hoping to be as helpful as they can be. There are pastors here and lay leaders, seminary professors and churchwide leaders and bishops. They are representative of the geographic, cultural, social, and racial diversity that characterize our church. They love the Lord. They love their neighbors. And they share a passion for helping us become who we say we are.

Will We Mean It?

If you keep your eyes open, you will notice a lot of signs out there that probably don't really mean what they say. My all-time favorite is the sign on the side of an electrician's truck that says, "Let us remove your shorts!"

But isn't it time for us to finally, really, mean what we say on our signs? We are the Evangelical Lutheran Church in America. Let's be who we say we are.

Sharing the Story

In this book, the chapter writers briefly share their faith in sections titled "Who I am in Christ ..." As you read these stories of faith, consider these questions:

• Who am I in Christ?

• How will I share my story?

Foundations for Engaging Evangelism

PART ONE

CHAPTER I

What in the World Is God up to?

Richard Bliese

Who I Am in Christ . . .

I am a professor and academic dean at Luther Seminary in St. Paul, Minnesota. I have worked as a missionary in Germany and Zaire, as a parish pastor in large and small churches in the United States, and as an advocate for refugees and Christian leaders from all over the world. One of the greatest privileges in the church, however, is when you are allowed to teach people how to become Christian leaders. It's a humbling experience. The biggest challenge when teaching leadership—no matter where you are in the world—is not only focusing on leadership skills, leadership techniques or leadership virtues, but also teaching leaders how to follow Jesus. This is the goal of all evangelism efforts. Until leaders learn how to follow the call to follow Jesus, that is, until they are evangelized themselves, everything else in the classroom is powerless.

What holds true for the student also holds true for the teacher. I have experienced that teaching theology without constantly learning and growing in discipleship is lame. Discipleship is the grandest of adventures. Hearing the good news time and time again is the only way God keeps me on the path. I enjoy being surrounded by honest Christian people who share the gospel with one another in a loving and supportive way. Hearing honest stories about what God is doing for people in Christ Jesus is what motivates me to teach and evangelize.

Fully trying to understand evangelism is like grabbing hold of a big fish. Just when you think you've got it, it slithers away. But there is nothing more important for Lutherans than engaging evangelism. Lutherans even carry *evangelical* in their church's name! Evangelism is too important for us, therefore, to let it get away. On the other hand, there are few aspects of church ministry that make us more nervous than the *E* word. No one is neutral when it comes to discussing evangelism.

This chapter will try to get a hold of evangelism within the context of everything that God is doing in the world. The problem Christians often have is that when we gaze at the big picture, evangelism can get lost. Our goal is to tightly grab hold of God's mission in the world in a way that embraces evangelism. This is holistic mission. It is the only way, in truth, to keep a hold of mission and evangelism during changing and challenging times. And, so, we begin Part One of this book here, by answering the question "What in the world is God up to?" In other words, what is God's mission?!?

This is where the story of evangelism begins to have spark and power.

Understanding mission begins with building a picture of God and God's activities in the world. First, you need to paint your own picture of God. Second, you need to discover the biblical picture of God's mission actions for the world. Third, you need to paint a picture of God in Christ so large that it includes the world. God's mission through Jesus begins when these pictures talk to one another. One picture just won't do! Bringing all these images together is like bringing together the positive and negative cables on a battery. When they meet, there's electricity—an explosion of power! This is where the story of evangelism begins to have spark and power, when our story and the biblical stories of God's mission in Jesus Christ meet and form a brand new picture of God as a missionary God for the world!

Drawing *Your* Picture of God

Absolutely central to engaging evangelism is understanding God's big mission in the world. And the first key to understanding God's big mission is being able to draw your own picture of God. Young children sketch fascinating images when given the assignment to "draw God." They pick up paper, pencils, and crayons to tackle this awesome assignment. These divine works of art can be quite revealing.

Years ago, such God-images would have been of grandfatherly figures sitting on heavenly thrones sporting long beards and white robes. Some children today draw their grandmothers. Others imagine God as a friend with whom they can play, or as their teacher, a pastor, a police officer, or the parent who is watching over them every day.

Internal pictures of God are fascinating to discover. They are deeply theological, and they are powerful motivators not only for children but for adults as well. Adults may hesitate to "draw God," but that doesn't mean we don't have a clear mental image of God functioning in our lives. It is this internal, spiritual picture that really drives us! We don't always consciously think about this picture or theologize about whether it is orthodox or not. Like the backdrop to any theatrical production, our divine images set the stage for our behaviors, attitudes, knowledge, habits, and activities.

Where do these pictures come from? Everyone has a different well of experience from which to draw. Strong personal experiences, family beliefs, cultural location, economic status, religious upbringing, friends, experts, educational background, and so on can all shape our God images. The deeper you look, the more you discover that everyone is a theologian.

Just as individuals carry around God images, so too do families, groups, and congregations. The reason your congregation acts the way its does — or fails to act at all! — is due to its collective picture of God. Here's how you can test this out in your own congregation. Hold a spiritual art fair. Encourage the members of your community to gather up crayons, chalk, pencils, and paints in order to draw a collective picture of God. At first, this art challenge will appear to create only huge headaches. "Just one picture!" everyone cries. "That's impossible. Can't we all make our own individual pictures?"

Now, there's some truth to these individual cries. But it is also true that congregations and other religious groups automatically form collective pictures of God over many years. When you join any religious group, a common picture emerges that governs the group's life together. These pictures determine how the group thinks, acts, and worships.

This congregational art project is not as odd as it may sound at first. It is doable. It is, in fact, one of the most important projects any congregation must undertake before even starting to "do" mission or engage evangelism. A congregation must first answer the question "What is God doing in the world?" before it starts to act. Painting a collective picture of God—one way or another—will greatly assist you in defining your congregation's mission.

Once your congregation has unveiled its picture of God's activities in the world (or named God's activities) you will be able to completely comprehend why the congregational members act—week in and week out—the way they do. Let's get more specific. It's really the picture of God that lies behind every activity of your congregation, from how you do worship to how you work in the neighborhood, from how you allocate budgetary funds to how you organize the fellowship time. Here are some features—among many—to look for in your picture:

- What does God look like?

- Where is God?

- Does God appear active or passive?

- Does God seem content or is God suffering?

- Is God playing a specific role in your picture? Is God a king, a servant, a doctor, a host at a party, an activist, a preacher, a lawyer, a judge, a shepherd, a teacher?

- Does your God stand for justice, mercy, healing, equality, happiness, peace?

Your picture shows how you view God's action in the world. This is traditionally called "the mission of God." Mission is first and foremost not about what we do, but about what God is doing. How you view *God's* mission will also affect how you and your congregation do *your* mission. Just check your congregation's calendar of events for the week. If your picture of God is one who is active with people who are poor, then your church will also do these same activities. If your picture of God is one who is hosting a banquet where everyone is invited, then you will follow suit. If God heals people, then you will want to heal people. If God acts justly or mercifully, then the congregation will strive to act justly or mercifully. (A note of warning: Some pictures of God actually lead toward human laziness. If your congregation mostly does *nothing*, you will probably need to work on changing your picture of God before you do anything else!)

So, what is your church's picture of God's mission in the world? Discover this picture and you will likewise discover your own congregation's attitude and approach to mission. Mission begins when we can picture God as a missionary God for the good of the world.

Biblical Pictures of God

Engaging evangelism begins with understanding the big mission of God. And the second key to understanding God's big mission is discovering the many and varied biblical pictures of God. No one picture is sufficient. In fact, limiting God's activities to only one biblical picture can either kill mission fervor or make Christians into real fanatics. In American history, for example, when the conquest stories in the Old Testament (in which Israel was ordered into the promised land to conquer it) were the only picture of evangelism, this one picture led to horrendous results. The new European settlers conquered Native Americans, pushing them off the land. This same story motivated missionaries in the early twentieth century to talk in military terms about "winning the whole world for Christ." It's not that this picture isn't biblical. It is. But, taken alone, it is dangerous. In fact, *any* one Bible story describing God's activities in the world, taken alone and out of context, can lead to perilous consequences.

So . . . how can you discover a collage of biblical pictures that will be helpful—not hurtful—in driving your congregation to good evangelism and mission practice? Two concepts here are essential: community and discernment.

First of all, the whole mission concept assumes that the Christian community has a divine calling TOGETHER. Empowered by the Holy Spirit, the church is God's special people formed and shaped into a missionary team whose calling is to participate in God's mission for the world. Jesus' call to mission is OUR calling, and it is OUR calling to figure out together. Evangelism and mission are team sports. This means that, as we explore biblical pictures of God's big mission, we will do it together.

Second, discovering the biblical pictures of God's big mission happens as we *read* the Bible, *pray, talk* about what we have read, and then together *discern* what God is up to. The Bible is the historical witness of God's mighty activities for the world. As Christian communities read, listen, reflect, and learn together, we will experience the inspirational and imaginative force of the biblical stories. More than having weekly Bible study groups, communal discernment means that congregations will be intentional about engaging in faithful and sustained conversation, affirming the activity of the Holy Spirit in their midst.

Lutherans need to know that Christians all over the world are uncovering fascinating pictures of God as a missionary God throughout

Which book of the Bible contains the best mission texts?

Most Christians expect the answer to be Matthew's Gospel because of the Great Commission (Matthew 28:19). But the answer is that the whole Bible is a mission text! Each book was written to engage the Christian community in addressing mission. If you don't read the Bible to discover the various dimensions and diversity of God's mission, you misread it. It's that simple!

Scripture. The more we read the Bible, the more we are motivated to tell the story in compelling ways. This is, for example, the message of Luke's Gospel. One of the first things the resurrected Jesus does is to walk together with his disciples on the way to Emmaus and interpret for them the meaning of Scripture (Luke 24: 13-35). Today, Jesus' ministry among us is the same. The resurrected Lord assists Christians as we read Scripture together so that we can discern God's big mission . . . and joyfully be a part of it!

God's Big Mission

Now take all of the Bible's pictures of God — and include your own picture of God. What do you have? One massive mission collage! This is God's big mission. Does God prioritize any of these activities? God is creating the world, sustaining life, working for justice, feeding the poor, healing the sick, forgiving sins, and much more! Must we be involved with everything God is doing? That would be too demanding, right? Shouldn't we be practical? The answer is no. God wants us involved in all God's missionary activities. No compromises! That's the promise we make at the baptismal font. We express this with a simple vow in the Affirmation of Baptism (*Lutheran Book of Worship*, Minneapolis: Augsburg Fortress, 1990, p. 201), a vow that is worth repeating every morning. This vow has many pictures of God's activities behind it:

> You have made public profession of your faith. Do you intend
> to continue in the covenant God made with you in Holy Baptism:
>
> to live among God's faithful people,
>
> to hear [God]'s Word and share in [God]'s supper,
>
> to proclaim the good news of God in Christ through word and
> deed,
>
> to serve all people, following the example of our Lord Jesus,
> and to strive for justice and peace in all the earth?

Because of the way Lutherans read the Bible, all of God's missionary activities are seen as twofold in nature. These two dimensions are so important that they are contained in the vow above. One dimension can be labeled God's "Big Mission," and the other can be labeled God's "Central Mission." God's big mission is creating and sustaining life. This job is so big that everyone is asked to participate. It is God's world-wide mission mandate that includes sustaining life, justice, peace, and mercy. There are no exceptions. If we obey God's call to do the big mission, God promises to bless us, our families, and our communities.

This may sound offensive or difficult to some people for two reasons. First, how can we be expected to do all that work? It's too much! We want to paint a smaller picture of God. How could God expect a small congregation, for example, to accept all of God's activities in the world? Healing, education, poverty, relationships, housing, guilt and shame issues, world conflict, environmental justice, ethnic tensions, sexual inequalities, family, government, abuse, racism, addictions, hunger, and so on. Come on, God, be reasonable! How big is *your* congregation's budget? How can we be held responsible for all these divine activities? God's big mission is simply too BIG for us. Can't we just pick and choose what we want to do? The Bible clearly says no. God calls us and our religious communities to accept all of God's big mission activities. Period.

Second, what does it mean that God calls ALL people to perform the big mission? Doesn't God only expect Christians to accomplish this work? Although this is what many of us believed for years, the biblical picture of God is quite different. Hebrews 11 describes people of "faith" who accepted God's mission mandate for their lives. This list mixes Jewish patriarchs and "pagan saints"—for example, Abel, Enoch, Noah, Abraham, Isaac, Rahab, Samson, and Gideon.

The Bible also includes the likes of Melchizedek, Pharaoh, Cyrus, the wise men, the Samaritan woman, a Roman centurion, Jews and Gentiles, murderers and prostitutes, sinners and saints; all were participating in God's mission. Even a donkey was given a mission voice (Numbers 22:28-30)! The Bible says that God uses all people, even from other religious traditions, to get God's big mission completed.

So then why do we need Christian mission at all? Although all people are called to participate in God's big mission—working for life, justice, peace, and mercy—this call to mission isn't really good news. Why? First, these tasks are too difficult for us. We need help. There is simply no way that we can accept all that responsibility for God's big mission in the world. A new kind of plan is needed.

> *God uses all people, even from other religious traditions, to get God's big mission completed.*

But there is a second problem. Be honest. We don't really want to do God's big mission, do we? We are like Jonah. We constantly rebel against God's leadership over our lives. We don't want to do God's big mission because, quite frankly, we have our own private agendas. This is as true for individuals as it is for congregations.

Congregations don't want to do God's big mission, either. The Bible calls this attitude toward God many things, including rebellion, disobedience, sin, alienation, pride. Before we can fully embrace God's big mission, our state of mind and heart has to be reformed and changed 180 degrees from hard to soft. This is forgiveness and it happens when we hear the simple story about God's love for us through the life, death, and resurrection of Jesus. This is God's special mission, the second dimension of the baptismal vow (check it out above). In fact, what God has done for us in Jesus Christ is so important that God declares this special mission now to be God's *central* mission to the whole world.

God has called a few people, Jesus' disciples, together to accept a special mission. God's gift to you is the call to follow Jesus as a new way to embrace God's big mission in the world. That's the vow we make at baptism. It's also the vow we are called to renew each and every day.

God's Central Mission

Your baptismal vow includes two distinct divine missions: God's big mission (God's missionary activity in the world) and God's central mission, which is evangelism. How does one then define evangelism as God's central activity in the world?

- Evangelism is telling the simple story of Jesus.

- Evangelism is telling the story of Jesus so that it is truly good news for people.

- Evangelism is good news that brings benefits to its listeners.

- Evangelism invites a response of faith.

- Evangelism is the way that God's Spirit assists us in embracing God's big mission.

Jesus is the heart and center of all God's mission activities in the world. This insight comes only through hearing the story of Jesus. No one can "faithfully" paint this picture of God's mission except by faith. Because Lutherans know the dangers *and* the promise associated with evangelism, it becomes essential to embrace evangelism in a way that keeps Jesus central to all mission activities. How do we do that?

All God's mission activities can be framed within three important evangelism models. These evangelism models are so important that Lutherans practice them every week in worship. It's our traditional way, dating back to the Reformation, of grasping all the complexities of God's missionary activities while keeping them centered in the message about the cross of Christ. These models center on baptism, communion, and sharing Jesus.

1. Baptism as a model for engaging evangelism

God calls me to accept God's missionary activity in the world as my own. This is a free gift that is truly amazing. When I receive the gift of salvation, I also receive both a new relationship with God and a call to accept God's missionary activity in the world. Accepting the relationship with God means also accepting the call to go where God is going and do what God is doing. This call is a call to follow the Crucified One, which means a call to new life every day.

2. Communion as a model for engaging evangelism

God calls me to be in a missionary team. Communion—which always implies a community!—is a call to teamwork. The word *team* has a double meaning. The "first team" is God. God is Father, Son, and Holy Spirit. Our call to the altar is a continual call to be in a relationship with the triune God. God's forgiveness makes this possible. But "the team" is also the church. I'm invited into this new *communal* team to live as God's missionary people. To be with God in mission means being with God's missionary people. God's forgiveness makes this teamwork possible.

3. Proclamation (telling the story) as a model for engaging evangelism

God's missionary team has the call to announce God's leadership over the whole world in Christ. This is a unique activity given only to the church. It is to announce and to embrace the message of the cross of Christ. Whereas we share many of God's missionary endeavors with other peoples, cultures, and religions, this one task is uniquely Christian. We declare God's leadership (God's reign) in the world in Christ Jesus.

Consequently, when Lutherans don't do evangelism well, they know instinctively that they have a "heart problem." If Jesus is at the heart of God's big mission in the world, then our "mission" problems are usually "evangelism" problems. Your congregation may need a heart transplant if your mission is out of focus. Is there something about the way you baptize, commune, and share Jesus' story that isn't setting people free for God's big mission? Do people in your congregation "get" God's mission picture?

Engaging evangelism will not result from a fresh wave of activism from clergy or laity, nor for some new hot program. Our greatest need is for a renewal of vision about evangelism and mission. Evangelism and mission are finally not about us "doing something." They are about the vision of the church as both the messenger and the embodiment of the message. God's mission in the world has a church. That's the biblical picture we are striving to discover! We are "church" because we have accepted identification with all God's big activities in the world through Christ. The church's role is not only to tell the story about Jesus, but to embrace the message in its lifestyle. We are called not only to proclaim a message, but to live it. That will mean finally that we will have to suffer with and bear the difficulties, hardships, and sins of those with whom we share the message of Jesus. That's our mission. We tell the story while living the life of a disciple of Christ. They go together. That's faith. That is engaging evangelism.

Summary

God's big mission includes all God's activities for the benefit of the world. It is one massive, divine, mission collage. And at the center of this big mission is God's central mission, which is evangelism. Engaging evangelism is about telling the story of Jesus in a way that is good news to people and that invites them to respond to the invitation to be a part of God's big mission in the world. Each one of us, as we receive the gift of salvation, is also given a call to proclaim that Jesus is central to God's big mission. No one else on the face of the planet has been given this specific task to both proclaim and embrace this good news about Jesus. But we do not do this alone. The church has been called as a special missionary team to fully enter into and accept God's big mission picture. In other words, God's central mission is carried out through *us*. Wow! What a mission! What a message! What a wonderful picture of God in the world.

For Reflection and Discussion

1. How would you paint a picture of God's activities in the world? How would your congregation paint this same picture? Is there a difference?

2. What images, ideas, and activities come to mind when you hear about "God's big mission"? That comes to mind when you hear the word *evangelism* or the word *gospel*?

3. As you read the Bible, how do you understand the story of Jesus as good news for people in your family? In your neighborhood? People in the poorest sections of your city? Friends in the hospital?

4. Does your congregation talk together while reading Scripture about the practice of evangelism in your community? If not, how might this happen?

5. What are the five most important Bible passages that have informed your congregation about how to understand and practice evangelism and mission in your context?

CHAPTER 2

How in the World Does God Get Stuff Done?

Robert Wallace

Who I Am in Christ . . .

As a young child I attended worship with my grandparents at First English Lutheran in Lockport, New York, where I learned the liturgy of the church at the tip of my grandfather's finger. During those years, an energetic pastor and the junior choir director each marked me with their love for the Lord and the church. After confirmation, I dropped out of active participation but occasionally attended worship and a citywide youth group. During five years at Davidson College, I experienced a spiritual awakening. The witness of a homemaker, involvement in Young Life, the birth of a campus Christian fellowship, and the biblical teaching and inspiring worship at Resurrection Lutheran in Charlotte, North Carolina, all contributed to my emerging identity as a disciple of Jesus Christ. During two visits to Koinonia Farms in Americus, Georgia, Millard Fuller and LaDon Sheets issued the challenge to examine the economic and societal implications of New Testament discipleship.

I planned to go to medical school, but graduated college with a B.A. in religion and set off to Gordon-Conwell Theological Seminary. I entered seminary without a sense of call but with questions regarding how to fit together my passion to engage others with the gospel, sense of responsibility to address poverty and injustice, and desire to give voice to a biblically based world view. I have a passion for spiritual growth, evangelism, and evangelical compassion and have spent 24 years in the Delaware-Maryland Synod (nine in the inner city), 18 months as the ELCA director for evangelism, and recently became senior pastor at Nazareth Lutheran in Cedar Falls, Iowa.

God is on a mission in this world, and at the very center of that mission is evangelism. God wants everyone to hear the invitation to new life! But how does God get this done? How does this happen in our world today? The Bible tells of God acting in mighty ways to restore relationships with people and bring the good news of Jesus. Most astounding of all, God raised Jesus from the dead. All these mighty acts might make us think that God always gets things done in the world through remarkable means, and that the Christian life is all about hanging on until God decides to act.

In the Bible, however, we also find many instances of God accomplishing something great not through mighty acts, but through ordinary people! God selects, shapes, and sends ordinary people, even people who — to us — seem the most unlikely for the job at hand.

God selects, shapes, and sends ordinary people.

In the Old Testament, for instance, God chose Moses, a murderer hiding from authorities and holding a low-paying job, to lead the Hebrew people out of bondage. God worked through David, a teenager who seemed to lack the athletic build and prowess of his older brothers, to defeat the champion of an opposing army. Later on, David even became Israel's ruler. In the New Testament, the apostle Paul found a ministry partner in a widow, businesswoman, and thriving entrepreneur named Lydia. She helped plant and lead the Christian movement in Philippi. Each of these examples shows God selecting ordinary — not perfect — people, shaping them, and sending them to accomplish God's work in the world. God got great things done through these ordinary people because each said yes to God's call, embraced this God-given vocation, and served God's plan.

The same holds true today. God expands the power of Jesus Christ in the world through the ordinary people God selects, shapes, and sends. The church has used the terms election, discipleship, and priesthood of believers to describe the ways in which God gets stuff done.

Selected to Live and Tell the Story

Most elections are all about winners and losers. The competition for votes is fierce. Money is lavished on professional advertising campaigns. Even at the most local levels, a candidate has to be willing to go the distance, putting everything she has into the process of getting elected. He needs to convince voters that he is the best — more trustworthy, more qualified, and more worthy than the next guy.

The election we are talking about here is different. People are not elected to be a part of God's mission because they are the most worthy or wonderful. In fact, the most unlikely people are often selected to carry out God's plan!

You may have heard, for example, the Hebrew (Jewish) people referred to as God's chosen people. This is because, in fact, God *did* choose this tribe for a special purpose. "For you are a people holy to the LORD your God . . . [chosen] out of all the peoples on earth to be his people, his treasured possession" (Deuteronomy 7:6). But just in case the people were tempted to be proud of this, God reminded them, "It was not because you were more numerous than any other people that the LORD set his heart on you — for you were the fewest of all peoples" (Deuteronomy 7:7).

God did not choose the Hebrew people because they were so special but, rather, because God had a special job for them to do. This all started thousands of years before Jesus was born, when God selected Abram and Sarai (later known as Abraham and Sarah) to follow a new direction, take on a new identity, and parent a new people. (Check out the whole story in Genesis 12-17.) This herdsman and his wife lived literally in the middle of nowhere. They weren't kings or high priests or wealthy landowners or famous philosophers. They weren't citizens, much less leaders, in one of great civilizations of ancient times, in Greece or Rome or Egypt or China. They were simple people, ordinary in every way, and as unlikely as you could imagine. And yet, God chose them and blessed them so that they would become a blessing to others. God told them straight out that their election was not for their own sake. It was part of God's plan to rescue the whole world. "All the families of the earth," God said to the wide-eyed Abraham, "will be blessed through you" (see Genesis 12:3).

Many years later, the promise that God would bless the whole world reached ultimate fulfillment when Jesus was born to Mary and Joseph, more ordinary people selected to help carry out God's plan. Through Jesus, the breach between God and humans has been repaired, and it has become clear that God's people have no geographic, racial, or cultural boundaries. Through the cross and resurrection, the power of sin, Satan, and death has been destroyed and these things can no longer keep people apart from the kind of life God gives.

In Jesus, God acted to restore people, to forgive, and to heal. And God wants every person on earth to know this! That is why, in our time, God gave birth to—elected!—the church so that it would act as God's agent, the body of Christ, in the world. Christians are those people who have received and embraced God's gifts in Jesus, and who are now called to live the story and tell the story, so that other people might come to faith and receive God's gifts. God will bless the nations (including your next-door neighbor, teammate, colleague at work) through baptized Christians who now make up the family of Abraham and Sarah's descendants. God calls you—an ordinary person!—through your baptism, to be a blessing to other people.

Writing to his friends in Ephesus, the apostle Paul makes this same point as he describes the human condition apart from God's election: We have no claim to God's love. We are not able to show God that we deserve anything except the death sentence that sin earns. (See Ephesians 2:1-3; and Romans 3:23 and 6:23.) It was rich mercy and great love that motivated God to rescue us and, through Christ, God shows us the "immeasurable riches" of God's grace (Ephesians 2:4-7). In other words, God makes it possible for us to receive what we do not deserve! God has done this in order to give us a new relationship—with God and with each other—through faith. God has given us a new life . . .

and this new life includes acting on God's behalf (Ephesians 2:8-10). God gives us—rescued people—both a new relationship and a new purpose. God uses us—ordinary people!—to accomplish extraordinary things. This is how God gets stuff done.

Bob's Story

Chances are good that your own experience of God has come not through some mighty or miraculous act, but rather through the words or actions of ordinary people. That's how it was for Bob.

On a Friday afternoon in late October, Bob needed a break from campus life and walked to Dwight and Anne's home. Dwight and Anne provided rides to church for students who attended the college in their small North Carolina community, and often invited students to visit them at home. Although it was an outstanding fall day with temperatures in the mid-60s and fall foliage at peak colors, Bob didn't notice. It had been a long week, adding to an already discouraging fall semester. High school hadn't been much fun; the grades

> *God uses us—ordinary people!— to accomplish extraordinary things.*

were pretty good, but that was one of the few positives in a life filled with discouraging words. College was supposed to be a new beginning for Bob, but he felt overwhelmed academically and shut out relationally. Just putting many miles between hometown and college didn't resolve his problems.

Over a glass of sweet tea, Anne and Bob chatted and then Bob chose to tell Anne what was really going on. Anne then asked whether Bob found any comfort and encouragement from the Lord. The response was a quizzical look, so Anne relayed how prayer during the tough times brought her calmness, insight, and strength.

Later, Bob couldn't remember exactly what Anne said, but during the walk back to campus, the tears flowed—tears of longing, because Anne revealed an intimate relationship with God that he had never known, and tears of hope, because in everyday language Anne asked God to guide him through the challenges and questions he faced. While sipping a glass of sweet tea, Anne introduced Bob to the great spiritual adventure, to life viewed through the lens of faith in Jesus Christ.

God gave Anne the ministry to introduce Bob to the kind of life God offers through Jesus Christ. What if Anne attempted to bolster Bob's sagging spirit with a pithy motivational proverb or assurances that everything would turn out okay? What if Anne felt insecure or uncomfortable telling her faith story and inviting Bob to look at the Christian life in a fresh way? What if Anne didn't pray? But Anne did listen, share her story, and offer prayer, and in so doing helped Bob experience God's love in a new and life-changing way. Anne was selected by God to do this work. And Anne did it.

Here's the kicker to this exchange. Years later, that day with Anne remains a special and lasting memory for Bob. Anne, however, can barely recall the discussion because, for her, talking to other people about God's love was a regular part of everyday conversation.

Through normal, everyday conversations between ordinary people, God brings those who currently live apart from God's promise and estranged from God's love to faith in Jesus Christ. Through our everyday actions, God works miracles. God elects us to live and tell the story. We are selected to be a blessing to the world.

Discipleship: Shaped to Live and Tell the Story

Can you imagine the scene?!? Eleven disciples stood there as Jesus began to give them their special instructions, the music from *Mission: Impossible* swelling in the background. "This is your mission," Jesus might have said, "should you choose to accept it." They had to be sweating bullets. But Jesus promised the disciples (and others who were certainly gathered with them) that he would be with them ALWAYS . . . even to the end of the age. And then he gave them what is often called the Great Commission.

God wants to use ordinary ME?!? But how do I know what gifts I have to offer?

Rick Warren, founding pastor of Saddleback Church in Lake Forest, California, uses the acronym SHAPE when referring to the unique way God engages each person in the mission of the church.

S represents the spiritual gifts given to everyone at baptism (see 1 Corinthians 12 and Romans 12).

H refers to the heart's passion. Each person has different interests and gets excited about different causes and issues. This is good because we live in a complex world.

A stands for abilities, the variety of different abilities God gives each person.

P refers to personality and the various qualities that go into this mix that has one person engaging relationships, work, and play in one way while someone else relates in a different way.

E represents a person's life experience. Our past influences the preferences we have and the choices we make today.

For example, God's gifts of healing and forgiveness bring reconciliation to past relationships, events, and circumstances that left us with wounds or bitterness. Sometimes the healing process takes time, but as the mending takes hold in our lives, the hurt from our past becomes an asset that enables us to have compassion for other people. Our experience shapes us so that we can be a useful part of God's plan.

Take these five facets all together and you get the SHAPE of a person. While we may have similarities to certain people, the fact of the matter is no two people are identical because God has shaped every person in a unique and wonderful way.

Now, although there are a LOT of places in the Bible where Jesus sent his followers off onto a special mission, this is probably the most famous. "Go therefore and make disciples of all nations," he told them (Matthew 28:19; see also parallel passages in Luke 24:44-49 and Acts 1:6-8). Before Jesus removed his visible presence, he commissioned his followers to tell the story of how God reclaims people through the cross and resurrection. But telling the story was only the beginning. These followers would also help new believers learn how to live as committed followers of Jesus Christ.

Disciple-making is that process through which God's chosen people—those ordinary people who are selected by God to be a part of God's central mission—discover both the unique way God has shaped them and what God has called them to do. At creation, God gave humans responsibility for the care of creation. By turning against God, humanity stepped outside of God's intention and could no longer do the work God had in mind for them. Election ends this separation and restores us to the relationship God intended. God chooses us ordinary people—rebellious and broken—to be a part of the special mission to restore all people to God through Jesus Christ. Responding in faith to God's election, we undergo this shaping process that God promises to do in the lives of all the elect. (See Philippians 1:6.) We become disciples of Jesus Christ, shaped by the Holy Spirit as we engage in worship, Bible study, small groups, service projects, financial giving, and evangelism.

The apostle Paul uses several different images to illustrate the shaping process of discipleship. Writing to his friends in Corinth, for example, Paul describes the shaping process as a triumphal procession and the spreading of fragrance (2 Corinthians 2:14-17). When a victorious army returned from battle in Paul's day, the city held a parade and lit large pots of incense along the route to fill the city with a sweet fragrance as a sign of triumph. Paul applies this image to the person who is captured by Christ and becomes a sign of Christ's victory to the world. A disciple's daily life becomes the fragrance of the new life in Christ. It is a "scent" that will attract those open to God's selection and shaping, and repel those who reject the gospel message.

Paul also describes discipleship as an unveiled face (2 Corinthians 3:12-18), making reference to a famous story from the Old Testament. You might remember that when Moses returned from his mountaintop encounter with God with the second edition of the Ten Commandments, his face was beaming because he had been talking with God. According to Paul, Moses put a veil over his face so the Israelites would not notice that the glow was fading. Paul contrasts Moses' experience with the new relationship with God that Jesus offers. When we live as a follower of Jesus Christ, the Holy Spirit puts us through a spiritual makeover that transforms our thoughts, attitudes, and behavior to be more and more like Jesus. Although we remain works in progress, God is shaping us and we can stop hiding behind a veil, pretending we're someone we're not. We can let people know what God is up to in our lives.

> **Although we remain works in progress, God is shaping us.**

Paul uses a common, everyday image when he says that a disciple is like "treasure in clay jars" (2 Corinthians 4:7). In his day, people put things of great value, like expensive ointments, coins, or jewels, in ceramic vases or other vessels that protected the property and honored its value. No sane person would ever consider putting something of great value in ordinary clay pottery because it easily chipped and broke. But God does the unexpected by entrusting to ordinary humans, with all our frailties, the things of greatest value—the gift of the knowledge of Christ and the call to share this gift with other people. Maybe we should display a bumper sticker saying, "I'm a cracked pot for Jesus!"

Finally, Paul says the people God selects and shapes—disciples—are sent into the world as ambassadors for Christ (2 Corinthians 5:20). Followers of Jesus Christ represent the reign of God's love in and for the world. Every day becomes an occasion for Christians to show and tell—showing God's gifts of love, compassion, reconciliation, and healing in our response to human suffering, and telling the story of Jesus and the difference he makes in our lives.

Paul uses these images and others to encourage his friends, and all who are selected and shaped by God, to be a part of God's central mission, giving witness to God's extraordinary mercy and grace through Jesus Christ. Our sincerity becomes the fragrance that evokes hope. Our perseverance, moral behavior, and trustworthy character glow in contrast to what people normally experience. Our handling of tough situations displays a strength of character and inner fortitude that sometimes surprises even ourselves. And our treatment of other people — the love and peace we offer — extends God's love and forgiveness.

This way of living is only possible because God wants that kind of life for us. Living according to our own whims and desires, we tend to stay hooked on ourselves. The risen Christ makes it possible for us to truly care for other people. Chosen and called at baptism, and shaped by the ongoing work of the Holy Spirit, we can carry out God's promise that we will be a blessing to all people. When in the course of everyday life we attend to the needs of other people, as disciples of Jesus, we experience true freedom. When our lives are truly shaped by Christ, we can experience the joy that comes from being a part of God's central mission in the world.

Cindy's Story

You have probably experienced the freedom and joy that comes as your life is shaped by Christ. Cindy did. Cindy was a mom with three kids who also worked part-time for a grocery store chain. Sunday and church were part of her upbringing and as an adult she helped out with Sunday school for young children. At church meetings, Cindy spoke passionately about helping teens to know and love Jesus. Her particular concern was how the congregation's confirmation program tended to turn teenagers away from the church instead of increasing their desire to follow Jesus.

When Cindy's pastor invited her to rebuild and lead the confirmation ministry in the congregation, her first response was, "No way!" She knew her preference for order and routine did not mix with the high-spirited energy and unpredictable emotions of middle-school youth. The pastor asked her to let the initial shock fade away and then check out where she sensed God leading. After a couple days of reflection and prayer Cindy said yes, with some reluctance and trepidation.

Immediately, God made use of her passion for teens, ability to organize, so-so personal experiences from confirmation, relational leadership, and spiritual discernment. The congregation's approach to confirmation changed so radically that students started to invite their friends. (Miracles do happen!) After they were confirmed, many of the teens wanted to come back to serve as high school guides, band members, and helpers.

God continues to do amazing things through ordinary people who trust God and put their faith in Jesus. God has selected and shaped YOU for participation in this big mission. And nothing you ever do will be more important or more wonderful.

The Priesthood of All Believers: Sent to Live and Tell the Story

While Paul uses an image from government life to describe our calling as ambassadors of God's love (2 Corinthians 5), Peter uses the example of an Old Testament priest to describe the way in which we are sent— as selected and shaped people of God—to be a part of God's central mission.

Now, most of us don't think of ourselves as priests, but that is what Peter says we are, every single one of us. "You are a chosen race," he says, "a royal priesthood, a holy nation, God's own people" (1 Peter 2:9). What could this possibly mean?!?

Well in those days, a priest went before God on behalf of the people and sometimes offered various sacrifices to express repentance, thanksgiving, or loyalty. The priest also went before the people on behalf of God to encourage rightful living. Jesus changed the role of priest from something restricted to people especially set aside for this work to the kind of life God wants all the baptized to live. This is what sixteenth-century reformer Martin Luther emphasized when he coined the phrase "priesthood of all believers." As priests, we go to God with our needs, aspirations, challenges, trials, and so on. We go to our neighbors to bring the good news, in both story and loving acts, that Jesus Christ is alive. We are priests whenever we serve as a bridge between God and people.

Peter knew that we are selected and shaped into priests for one reason: So that we can be SENT into the world. "You are a chosen race," he said, "a royal priesthood . . . in order that you may proclaim the mighty acts of him who called you out of darkness into his marvelous light" (1 Peter 2:9).

Zach's Story

God gets things done by selecting, shaping, and sending ordinary people into the world. People like Zach.

Zach manages a busy music store. Few of his employees are over 30. Most wear a lot of black and metal. You would need more than a couple of hands to count all the piercings, and the favorite tattoo in the shop appears to be a skull and crossbones. But these young guys love Zach. You can tell. He treats them with respect. He talks with them about their favorite bands. He honors their (pretty amazing) knowledge of instruments and equipment. Zach will be the first to tell you that he doesn't like church. But he has found one that welcomed him. In fact, he plays in the worship band about once a month. He has heard something at this church that has gotten his attention. And he is being shaped by it. Now, here's the really awesome part of the story: All of those young guys in the store . . . they know that Zach is going to church these days. He talks about it! They know he plays in the band. And they are curious. If they were invited, probably some of them would come. Before too long, Zach will get around to asking them.

He may or may not know it yet, but Zach is a priest. He is a bridge between God and those young guys in his store. He has been selected by God to be a part of God's central mission. He is being shaped by the

Holy Spirit through the things he is experiencing at his church. And he has been sent right into that store, right into those young lives, to live and to share the story of what God has done to rescue the whole world through Jesus.

Summary

How does God get stuff done in the world? God uses ordinary men and women to be a part of the central mission, to share God's love for humanity through story listening and telling, loving acts, and invitation. The God who created distant galaxies, the human genotype, music, colors, and all the other wonders of creation, chooses to convey the message of amazing grace through every baptized person. You and I, cracked and chipped as we may be, are by God's decision and the Spirit's inspiration ambassadors of God's love and priests to our neighbors. Evangelism, therefore, is not a church program finally assigned to some folks who didn't say no. Rather, it is the way of life for all the baptized. God gets stuff done in the world through us!

For Reflection and Discussion

1. How did you first learn about Jesus? What ordinary people were involved?

2. As you look over the course of your life, who has helped you mature as a Christian disciple? How did these people influence you?

3. Do feel hesitant talking to other people about God's love and the kind of life Jesus offers? If so, why? If not, what has helped you to do this?

4. How have you experienced God getting stuff done through you? Describe your role or calling to carry out God's central mission, which is evangelism.

5. How might congregations design their mission and ministry to support God's work through the everyday life of ordinary Christians?

CHAPTER 3

What Is God up to in Our Lives?

Kathryn Bradley-Love

Who I Am in Christ . . .

I am an evangelist seeking people already equipped or willing to train and work for the building of the kingdom of God.

I am an energetic speaker who is unapologetically influenced by members willing to "make Christ known for the healing of the world" (in the words of themes from the ELCA Evangelism Team and Lutheran World Federation).

I am a bridge builder who seeks spiritual renewal and discipleship for both laity and clergy, and a cultural awareness for congregations open and willing to inspire youth leaders.

My goal is to reach lay people with the messages of evangelism and prayer while bridging the gap between the church and its community. I serve as the Associate Director for Evangelism in the ELCA and continue to give form to the model of evangelism that calls all to discipleship.

God's central mission is evangelism — telling the story of Jesus and inviting people to respond by answering the call to participate in God's big mission. The central mission is carried out by ordinary people like you and me. But God can't use us to tell the story until we have a story of our own to tell.

What's your story? What is God up to in *your* life?

The apostle Paul got to tell his story again and again. It happened, for example, every time he got arrested and had to explain himself. In those situations, he discovered that his story — the one about how Jesus met him on the road to Damascus and called him to turn his life around — was all he really had in his defense. He told King Agrippa that when Jesus appeared to him, he asked, "Who are you, sir?" "And the Lord answered, 'I am Jesus whom you are persecuting. But get up and stand on your feet; for I have appeared to you for this purpose, to appoint you to serve and testify to the things in which you have seen me and to those in which I will appear to you" (Acts 26:15-16, *Holy Bible, New Living Translation*).

How could your life and purpose stay the same if you encountered Christ on a road in your community, similar to Paul's experience on that road to Damascus? Why might God choose to meet with you? More importantly, how would you react during that remarkable moment?

The dream I am about to share with you is unique. This is my own personal story, the story of how I was encountered by Christ. It is different from Paul's story and from yours. But, by my telling it, I hope to inspire you to discover what God is up to in your life.

Most dreams are filled with detail, but not this one. The entire dream was so brief — it felt like it lasted about 30 seconds. There were no angelic images or chimes with music; no radiance in the skies; no chariots, tents, coliseums, change-makers, markets, or sounds of animals. It was not a setting reminiscent of the time when Christ walked the earth. The time seemed to be today, as if Christ made a special journey just to visit me. During the dream I experienced nothing outstanding or miraculous; nothing appeared out of the ordinary. There on the road, it was just Christ and me. I did not see his face, so I cannot describe his features. Like meeting a friend, I was just there to hear his message. We were in conversation, and I experienced a real, gentle presence as I took instructions on this path. Suddenly, either from his robe or his side, Jesus handed me what appeared to be a small package. I realized it was for me. It had simple wrapping with a plain ribbon. As he gave it to me, he said these three words: "Hold the box." And even as I reached out to take it, I knew that, by receiving it, my answer was "Yes, Lord." Yes to all the contents. Yes to the call. Yes to all the blessings and all the struggles that answering his call would mean. Yes, without reservation.

> **Something HAPPENS to us when we are met by God through Jesus Christ.**

That is how my story begins. Your story is different. But, however the story goes, the outcome is the same. Something HAPPENS to us when we are met by God through Jesus Christ. We are accepted just as we are, loved and forgiven, no matter how terribly we have been living our lives. Just ask Paul! And we are given a new purpose in life, to be "servants and witnesses" to Jesus. We are given something to boast about and set free to make a difference. We are continually transformed by Christ's love and shaped into missional communities. It may not come to you on the roadside in a blinding vision or all wrapped up in a box, but it is really and truly the most amazing gift any of us could possibly receive.

God Gives Us Something to Boast About

Here is one of the things God is up to in our lives: God gives us something to boast about. One of the reasons so many of us fail to hear or see God at work in our ministries and lives is the belief that God only speaks to the chosen. "Who am I to hear God's voice?!" we ask. "What would God want with me?!" We accept the biblical stories about how God comes to meet people because, well, they are stories in the Bible! They seem to belong to some long ago time and place. We believe they couldn't possibly have anything to do with us today. But we are wrong. God has chosen us!

For example, when we read about how God showed up to tell Abraham and Sarah that they would begin a whole new life and give birth to a new nation at the ripe old age of 100, we accept the account because it is biblical. We don't see these two old people as *real* people. We imagine that they must have been much holier, much more faithful than we are. And, since we cannot imagine having the faith of Abraham or the fortitude of Sarah, we struggle to see ourselves as chosen and set apart.

"Surely," we say, "God is not birthing a nation in me!" But, remember, both Abraham and Sarah laughed when God showed up. They could hardly believe it either!

The word we share is not about us. It is about what God is doing through us.

Recently, I had the opportunity to lead a cross-cultural evangelism conference. During the question-and-answer time, one woman raised several concerns about her ability to do evangelism. "How," she asked, "can I evangelize when I do not feel that I know enough? How can I know I am worthy to share with others?" She added, "I have not yet fixed my life, and the people that I minister to might know of my struggles. I feel strange speaking to others when my joy is not complete. Who am I to tell them about Christ?" She didn't laugh at the thought that God might be calling her to carry the good news; this thought made her feel unworthy and afraid.

Now, you can probably think of several answers to her questions. They certainly became a focus of discussion that day. We finally all agreed that none of us can fix our own stuff. But God can . . . and will! For that reason, the word we share is not about us. It is about what God is doing *through* us.

When we meet God through Jesus Christ, we meet a God who sees all of our brokenness and all of our weaknesses and all of our faults. God sees all of the reasons why we shouldn't be worthy of the call to follow. And God loves us anyway. God forgives us. God chooses us! And we are called to be a part of the important work God is doing in the world. This is the amazing gift that God first gives to us as we are welcomed in the waters of baptism. And, when we baptize babies, it is especially clear that this is a GIFT. It is given to us before we can do or say anything to earn or deserve it. Furthermore, this is a gift that, amazingly, we receive again and again. It comes to us as we hear the Word. It fills us up as we are fed at the Lord's Table. God comes to meet us, right in the middle of our often very messy lives, and says, "Come, follow me. And I will make you fishers for people. I will give you lives filled with meaning and purpose. I have selected you, and I will shape you and send you out to be a part of what I am doing."

The apostle Paul knew that he didn't deserve God's call to follow. He was out persecuting Christians the day Jesus showed up. That's why he spent his whole life joyfully boasting about what God had done in his life. In 1 Corinthians 1:27-31, his boast was not out of arrogance, but out of thanksgiving:

> God chose what is foolish in the world to shame the wise; God chose what is weak in the world to shame the strong; God chose what is low and despised in the world, things that are not, to reduce to nothing things that are, so that no one might boast in the presence of God. He is the source of your life in Christ Jesus, who became for us wisdom from God, and righteousness and sanctification and redemption, in order that, as it is written, "Let the one who boasts, boast in the Lord."

Paul didn't mind boasting about what God had done in his life. And, strange as it may sound, boasting is one of the tools we have as we share the good news about Christ and the stories about what he means to us. We dare to boast, not because God is finished with us or because we are "fixed." We boast in the Lord, who somehow manages to take people who are *not* finished and *not* fixed, and use us anyway.

God Sets Us Free to Make a Difference

Every once in a while, we are blessed with an experience that brings life into focus and we see clearly what the point of it all is. I had one of those experiences one semester when I was enrolled in a class titled "Death and Dying." One of the outside projects was to visit a morgue.

Staring down into the laboratory through the window of the observation deck, a classmate and I saw the remains of a 69-year-old male. As the instructor spoke to the medical students who were participating in the autopsy below, he turned the microphone on and extended an invitation to my new friend and I to come into the laboratory.

"Ladies, come on down and have a closer look," he said. "You'll never be the same."

We did not move, so the invitation was repeated.

"Come on down," he said, grinning at us.

Together we went down the stairs, holding hands like two four-year-olds. We had only just learned each other's names, but we had become hand-holding friends. I think she was shaking! Maybe I was shaking just a little too!

We entered the laboratory where students were studying body organs, and the instructor explained what we saw as he led us around the lab. I managed to ask what caused this particular death: liver cancer. I asked to see the cancer in the liver and a medical student directed my eyes by pointing as she was working. When we finished hearing the details, we headed for the door. I took a deep breath, as did my newly acquired friend. We finally released each other's hands! And I knew the instructor had been right. I would never be the same.

We had, in fact, seen death in its fullness. And, in death, we had seen life. That man was someone's husband, someone's father, someone's friend. A few days later, those who loved him would view him and bury him and weep because he was gone. I couldn't help wondering if he had fulfilled all of his potential and accomplished his purpose. Had he known that we are called to be in a real relationship with God and with one another? Did his life inspire changes in others during his journey? Did he take the opportunity to tell his story? Is the world a better place because he was here? Was he baptized and, if so, how did

We are saved by grace and not by any work of ours. Isn't it "un-Lutheran," then, to say that we have to DO something (especially something as hard as evangelism)?

Well . . . no! Martin Luther knew from reading the Bible that the gift of salvation can never be separated from the call to discipleship. We serve and share and witness, not so that God will love us more, but because God loves us so much! God loves us enough to call us out of our old life of death and sin and meaninglessness . . . and into a new life of freedom and purpose and joy . . . into a life spent following Jesus and giving ourselves away for the sake of others. That's what salvation is all about. We don't have to DO anything to get it, but once we have it, we can't DO enough!

—*Kelly A. Fryer*

he live out his baptism? Did he boldly boast in the Lord? Did he answer God's call to make a difference?

Let me be clear: There is nothing this man could have done to make God love him more. Writing in his pivotal essay "The Freedom of a Christian" (*On Christian Liberty*, Fortress Press, 2003), Martin Luther reminds us of this. Famous for kicking off the Protestant Reformation, which led to the formation of the Lutheran church, Luther was writing some 500 years ago, so his language may sound a bit strange to us. (Where he writes "men," for example, read "people"!) But his message is as helpful today as it ever was. Through Christ, God loves us and saves us and sets us free. No work of ours, no effort, could accomplish this. In fact, the closer we get to Christ, the more we realize it. "The moment you begin to have faith," Luther wrote, "you learn that all things in you are altogether blameworthy, sinful, and damnable" (p. 8). Our freedom is a gift from God to us through Jesus Christ.

But the freedom we have in Christ is not for our sakes alone.

Christ sets us free *from* a life spent painfully and anxiously having to earn God's love . . . *for* a life spent joyfully worshiping God and serving our neighbor. Again, according to Luther (*On Christian Liberty,* p. 52):

> Although the Christian is thus free from all works, he ought in this liberty to empty himself, take upon himself the form of a servant, be made in the likeness of men, be found in human form, and to serve, help, and in every way deal with his neighbor as he sees that God through Christ has dealt and still deals with him.

Knowing that Christ has loved us and saved us and set us free in spite of ourselves, we give ourselves wholly over to serving our neighbors—both enemies and friends—and witnessing to the love of God. We are set free for engaging evangelism! We are set free to tell the story.

This is the difference that we are set free to make. This is what gives our lives purpose and meaning. This is our call.

God Never Stops Working on Us

We are chosen to be a part of God's mission in the world and set free to make a difference. But we should not think for a moment that this is a once and for all, one time only event. The truth is that we each need to hear this call again and again. Daily, we find ourselves wrestling with God and turning away from the call to serve and to witness. Daily, we need to repent of this sin and experience Christ's forgiveness. Daily, we need to be set free! In *The Book of Concord: The Confessions of the Evangelical Lutheran Church* (Minneapolis: Fortress Press, 2000, p. 452), Luther explains:

> Although we have God's Word and believe, although we obey and submit to his will and are nourished by God's gift and blessing, nevertheless we are not without sin. We still stumble daily and transgress because we live in the world among people who sorely vex us and give us occasion for impatience, anger, vengeance, etc. Besides, the devil is after us, besieging us on every side . . . so that it is not possible always to stand firm in this ceaseless conflict.

"The new life," Luther writes, "should be one that continually develops and progresses" (*The Book of Concord*, p. 469). In other words, God isn't finished with any one of us just yet.

Knowing that we ourselves are in need of God's ongoing transformation prevents us from ever being arrogant as we engage in evangelism. We know that *Christ came to save the lost!* And that includes every single one of us. We need Christ's daily forgiveness. We know that, in some ways, we need to be evangelized as much as the next person! In fact, this is one of the things that is sort of unique about doing evangelism as a Lutheran. We know that what we have to offer to the world is exactly the SAME thing that we ourselves need every day . . . the forgiveness, love, and freedom that only Christ can bring. *We can't possibly participate in Christ's mission to reach the lost . . . unless we ourselves are being reached by Christ.* That is why we gather for worship. That is why we dig into Scripture, listening for God's Word to us in Bible reading and study. That is why we pray.

Bishop Mark Hanson has called the ELCA to be a praying church because only a church at prayer will be able to be a church in mission. Only as we are transformed by the love and forgiveness of the God we meet in Word and Sacrament will we be instruments of transformation in our churches and in our world. Bishop Hanson writes the following in the final chapter of *Faithful Yet Changing: The Church in Challenging Times* (Minneapolis: Augsburg Fortress, 2002, p. 73):

> I have saved prayer for the last chapter of this little book, not because it is the least important, but because it undergirds everything else that we do. . . . The basic question is, "How do we stay renewed for our mission in the world?" We simply can't do it unless we are daily in the word, regularly at the Lord's table, faithfully among the gathered community, and in the presence of God in personal and corporate prayer.

The transformation of our world will begin as our churches are transformed. And the transformation of our churches, into centers of mission filled with evangelical passion, will only begin as you and I are transformed—every day!—by the God who meets us in prayer.

I challenge you, if you have not already done it, to put prayer on the front burner in your heart. There is a lot of debate about the role that prayer ought to play in our nation's schools. But, frankly, I have a much deeper concern. I am worried about what I observe to be a virtual absence of prayer in our *homes*. Years ago, prayer was a common practice in the home. Home is where children first learned the lessons of answered prayers. How did we manage to allow such an important practice to become nearly extinct—with the possible exception of a quickly muttered table grace? It is time to recover the practice of daily prayer with our families and in our homes. It is time to allow Christ to teach us how to live together, serving others and witnessing to God's love. I am pretty sure that we have forgotten these basic things. For example, I was delighted to learn from a woman I recently met that of her four adult children, two are college graduates, and one is in college right now. Another child is married, living in a prestigious community. It didn't occur to me until the conversation was over that she never said a single word about the relationship any of her children have with God.

We live in a culture that encourages us to trust in and celebrate our own wisdom and strength, our riches and might. Even in the church, we sometimes get confused and think that we are somehow better than other people (especially people who don't go to church!) because of what we "have" (that is, Jesus). But, as Jeremiah 9:23-24 tells us, the word of the Lord has something entirely different to say:

> Thus says the LORD: Do not let the wise boast in their wisdom,
> do not let the mighty boast in their might, do not let the wealthy
> boast in their wealth; but let those who boast boast in this, that
> they understand and know me, that I am the LORD; I act with
> steadfast love, justice, and righteousness in the earth, for in these
> things I delight, says the LORD.

God selects, shapes, and sends us to make a difference in this world. But that does not mean our story is over. In fact, it is just beginning. Once we answer Christ's call to be his servants and witnesses, we realize that there is nothing we could ever do to actually deserve this call. We need to be forgiven every day. Each day we are called and set free for service and witness. We ourselves need to be evangelized before we can be evangelists! We need to be transformed—converted—every single day in order to be instruments of transformation in the world. And this transformational process begins as we are in prayer.

> **We ourselves need to be evangelized before we can be evangelists!**

God Shapes Us into Purposeful Communities

Living in an individualistic society, as we do, it would be easy to assume that everything we have been talking about so far is "personal." And it is. Nothing is more personal than meeting Jesus Christ and hearing his call to follow him! But there is nothing "private" about any of this. When we are met by Jesus, we become members of his body, the church.

Think about this: The first thing that happened to Paul, after he was knocked for a loop by Jesus on the road to Damascus, was that he was brought into the community of believers through the brave testimony of a Christian named Ananias (Acts 9). Representing the community, Ananias went to Paul—even though he was scared half to death—and baptized him, bringing him into the community of faith. From the very beginning of the story, it has been clear: We do not practice faith alone. We are brought, through our encounter with Jesus, into a community of people who share a common purpose and who fulfill that purpose together.

Summary

I'll be honest: If you were to meet Jesus on the road today, I am not exactly sure what he would say to you. If you were to receive a wrapped gift box from Jesus, I am not exactly sure what would be in it. Your situation and the exact nature of your call are different from mine.

But I do know this. We are each given something to boast about. God is at work in us and through us! It is our job to participate in God's central mission, which means telling the story — *our* story — and inviting the world to respond. Christ chooses us and sets us free to make a difference, to be his servants and witnesses. But we do not do this alone. Through Jesus, God calls us into communities of purpose where we are daily transformed in order to be instruments of transformation within those very communities, and in the world.

For Reflection and Discussion

1. In order to tell the story, we have to have a story. Boast a little. What was your life like before you knew God was in it? How has following Jesus changed you? What HAS God been up to in your life? And what difference has it made for you?

2. What do you think is the real meaning of life? What gives your life purpose? How could "telling and living the story of Jesus" give direction to your life?

3. Our stories aren't finished being written yet. God is still at work on us. What areas of your life are still in need of transformation? Where are the growing edges for you, in your faith life?

4. What do you think about the claim that our faith is very personal, but can never be private? What difference does it make that you belong to a "public" community — the church? How does it strengthen your faith and make you more ready to tell the story to others? In what way is Christ calling you to go public with your faith right now?

CHAPTER 4

What Is God up to in the Church?

Dave Daubert

Who I Am in Christ . . .

Like a lot of Americans of my generation, I grew up in a caring family that gave me a strong foundation in many areas of my life. But church life was not a major part of my childhood, and my dad's parents had become inactive in church, so I was in the third generation of unchurched people. I have since discovered that I was not alone.

It was in college that two friends from the dorm, Scott and John, regularly invited me to attend Saturday worship with them. They were persistent in this, regularly inviting me but never pushing me to come with them every week. I finally agreed to join them, and there they introduced me to a God who I knew little about. Of all the people I met in college, Scott and John changed my life the most because God used them to introduce me to Jesus.

Eventually, I discovered that no one has a better theology about how God comes to us in Jesus than Lutherans. Lutherans know that Jesus comes to us through faith as a gift. Lutherans know that people matter to God and that God's love in Christ is intended for everyone. I now serve as the ELCA Executive for Renewal of Congregations.

Meeting Jesus eventually changed almost everything about how I saw the world. It also gave me a sense of how important it is that others meet Jesus, too. And because God used two people who loved both God and me enough to want us to meet, I am not the same person I was. That's the key to who I am, and it's the reason I do what I do.

Engaging evangelism really does begin with the story you and I have to tell. But we are not in this alone. We are part of a community — the church — that shares the unique responsibility of telling the good news about Jesus, who is at the very center of God's big mission in the world. What does the church need to look like in order to do this well? How is God transforming the church today so that it can tell THE story through which God will change the world? What would the church be doing if it really was the church God has called it to be? These are questions we need to be asking as we begin to realize that the church has entered a strange new day.

Take, for example, Don and Phyllis. They didn't grow up together, but their childhood experiences were much the same. Both had fathers who served in World War II and mothers who stayed at home. Both were brought to church to learn to be respectable people. It was in church that dominant community values were communicated. For this service their parents came to church, put money in the plate, and supported pastors and church buildings.

At the time, even unchurched people had some idea of what they thought God was doing in the congregation. The assumed answer was, "Helping people be respectable citizens." Church was at society's center, and respectable people went to church (or at least associated with it).

As Don and Phyllis grew up, North American culture went through rapid changes. The world quickly became less unified and more diverse. Society's center was less clear and the church's role was less clear, too. Don and Phyllis decided church was irrelevant and a waste of time.

Don and Phyllis got married (in a church) and had their children baptized (to appease grandparents) but never brought them to church. Their oldest daughter is a single mother of two. Her children haven't been baptized. They are the third generation of unchurched people in their family. With regard to the church, they will probably not "just drop in." They have no idea what they would be dropping in on.

It is a strange new day to be church. What exactly *is* God up to here?

God Is Serious about Conversion

A major flaw in the church life that Don and Phyllis were raised in was assuming that being Christian meant being like everyone else. Church life reinforced the cultural norms rather than calling forth values that were grounded in God's dream for the world. Being in church was not about making people new as much as it was about making them "normal."

This isn't the only way. The Augsburg Confession, written in 1530, laid out the basic theology of the Lutheran reformers. In it, the first four articles focus on God's commitment to a sinful world and to the work of Jesus Christ, given as a free gift and received through faith. Then Article V says, "So that we may obtain this faith, the ministry of teaching the gospel and administering the sacraments was instituted" (*The Book of Concord,* p. 41). The outcome of ministry is faith. Lutherans knew that evangelism—which tells the story about Jesus and invites people to respond in faith—was the starting point!

The first fruit of faith is a changed life.

After pointing to faith in Christ as the starting point, Article VI describes the "New Obedience." It says, "They teach that this faith is bound to yield good fruits and that it ought to do good works commanded by God on account of God's will and not so that we may trust in these works to merit justification before God" (*The Book of Concord,* p. 41). The reformers recognized a simple truth: The first thing a Christian does when the free gift of salvation is given is to answer Christ's call to participate in God's special mission, serving and witnessing and sharing for the sake of the world. *The first fruit of faith is a changed life.*

I am embarrassed to remember that shortly after I joined the Lutheran church in college, a friend said, "I suppose now that you're going to church you'll start acting different."

I responded, "No. I'm still the same old me."

In joining the church, no one had engaged me about discipleship. It was assumed that joining the church was the goal rather than one part of something more complete. I learned later that being a Christian means not only having a faith but also living a faith. Being a disciple of Jesus also involves *doing* Christianity. Faith changes people.

And those people are gathered into the church. The article called the "New Obedience" is immediately followed by Article VII, which describes the church. It is, according to the reformers who penned this important document, "the assembly of saints in which the gospel is taught purely and the sacraments are administered rightly" (*The Book of Concord,* p. 43). The church is, in other words, a new community. It is grounded in the faith and transformation in the lives of those who trust in Jesus' work. People who are called are called to be different. And they are called to community.

The fruit of hearing the gospel is faith. The life of faith brings with it a changed life. And people whose lives are changing form a community of people who are in the process of becoming different, marked with the cross of Jesus and committed to new values shaped by God's kingdom. Unlike the churches where Don and Phyllis were raised (or the one that I first joined), one would expect such a church to be supporting and training people who are being transformed instead of hoping to be like everybody else. Today, God is calling the church to get serious about conversion.

Conversion is the move from unbelief to disciple. It is the move from the "old" you to a "new" you, in Christ. For some people, this begins

Look at This!

The Augsburg Confession shows how to move from the "old" you to a "new" you.

Conversion = faith in Christ + changed life + connection to the church
                    (Article V)   (Article VI)   (Article VII)

with a dramatic experience. For others, it happens along the way, as they are raised and nurtured within the community of faith. For all of us, it is an ongoing process that continues throughout the whole course of our lives. And it includes three essential elements: faith, changed life, and connection to the church.

In the end, if Don and Phyllis are to return to church, then the church will have to stop taking faith for granted and stop thinking that joining the church means staying like everybody else. It will restore the notion that conversion is important, that faith changes lives, and that gathering believers is about affiliating with a community committed to being a part of something new where God is at work.

God Sets Us Apart

In Matthew 16:13-19, Jesus asks his disciples, "Who do people say that the Son of Man is?" They give him all sorts of responses. But Peter says, "You are the Messiah, the Son of the living God." And Jesus tells him, "On this rock I will build my church." The church is based not on what society says, but on faith in Jesus. By now, it should come as no surprise that the church is formed by faith and not the dispenser of faith.

The Greek word for church used in the New Testament (*ekklesia*) literally means "called out from." It represents a kind of separation—this group is set apart and unique. They gather out of their identification through faith with Christ. This is no ordinary group of people getting together.

Such an assembly is not just a mirror of the world around it. Christ stands at the center of this community. Transformed by faith and living out a vision of God's dream, these people represent a glimpse of a different kind of world. Their life together reflects this in their worship and praise of the God who claims them. In Scripture, preaching, and teaching, this community hears from the God who has called them. They gather at the baptismal font and the altar to celebrate God's presence in their midst. In relating to each other, they do so as forgiven people who are reconciled with each other in Christ. In making decisions, they are a prayerful people, both speaking and listening to God. In a very real way, the church is called to be clear about its unique identity as the body of Christ and call people forth from the world to new life.

My family moved a few years ago and we visited several congregations before agreeing on one to join. Most places subtly (one place not so subtly) conveyed a message that said, "Our members are nice people. Being a member is easy. You take one class (we even feed you lunch) and then you get up and say the creed (you can bring your hymnal up with you)."

The message was clear: "Joining this church is not going to change your life." These congregations had forgotten that changing lives was the first fruit of faith in Christ. In the process they had allowed their gathering to simply be a reflection of everything else in their world. In some important ways, they had missed what it means to be the church.

If people are going to take church seriously again, then the church will need to take itself seriously again. I meet too many people who have had the seeds of faith dashed by such congregations. If meaningful conversion means becoming a part of a community of faith, complacent churches will remain major barriers to discipleship far too often.

God Has a Dream for Us

Since the church is not about certifying that people are ordinary but about supporting people who in Christ are being made extraordinary, then today's congregation needs to find some purpose other than "we train respectable citizens." Society isn't sending people to the church for respectability training. "Please help us keep society stable" has been replaced by "We don't much care what you do in those buildings."

But there is good news. Rather than the world deciding what the church should be, the church is again free to ask, "God, what would you have us be?" The answer to that question may not restore the church to society's center, but it will free the church to discover a new missional presence in a world that has domesticated the Christian story or pushed its message to the fringes.

How can a congregation figure out what God's vision for it is?

You can begin by reading the book of Acts together. Talk about it. Pray about it. And, together, answer this question: Based on what you've read in this book, what was God's purpose for the early church? Why should you do this? God's purpose for THAT church is the same as God's purpose for YOURS. Based on this work you do together, write a purpose or vision statement for your church. You'll say it in your own way, from your own context. But the main idea is the same for EVERY church. The church is called out to be a part of God's big mission and, uniquely, to be a part of God's central mission: engaging evangelism!

—*Kelly A. Fryer*

Hoping to grow the church, the ELCA passed a decade-long evangelism strategy in 1991. Although the strategy failed in many respects (throughout the 1990s the church shrunk), we were able to learn a lot about the church by evaluating its effects. Not every congregation in the ELCA struggled. Some were doing amazing things. What was the difference between congregations that adapted to the new reality and those who floundered?

Congregations that were effective in reaching a world that didn't want to be reached were clear about their purpose. When members of the growing congregations were asked, "Why do you exist?" people knew the answer. Unlike many dying congregations, these churches ask, "If God is doing something in the world, how can we be useful to God in getting that done?" They have a sense of vision and the will to pursue it.

This takes a renewed sense that in a pluralistic and secular culture, what God is doing through the crucified and risen Jesus really matters. Scripture is clear that God is working in Jesus Christ to reconcile the whole world. But the church that Don and Phyllis left assumed that everyone knew about Jesus and the local world was OK. Reaching out didn't seem that important. Today, most people aren't against reaching out in theory. But new people mean major changes, and many congregations simply don't have the heart for that.

A congregation that understands its purpose has wrestled with God's dream for its mission and its people. This can mean months of prayer, Bible study, and dialogue. It takes strong leaders because some may choose to leave for something more comfortable. Often someone needs to risk taking the lead because when a congregation gets stuck, God uses changed people to change churches.

Today it is clear that *every* congregation needs to energetically claim, "God's purpose for our congregation is _____." Without that, nothing else is likely to make a difference. We get to participate in what God is doing. God is a missionary God and one of the first things that God is doing in the congregation is forming a purposeful and missionary people.

God Takes Every Place Seriously

The first chapter of John's Gospel reminds us that a basic tenet of Christian faith is that, in Christ, God has come down to dwell among us. This is called *incarnation* and it reminds us that Christ lives within and among those to whom he comes. What was removed and somewhat mysterious without Christ becomes concrete and tangible in the person of Jesus. Furthermore, in its setting, every congregation is called to look like Jesus.

This is essential for understanding congregations. People are joined to Jesus in baptism and enter into the church. When the congregation gathers, Jesus Christ speaks a living Word in Scripture and in proclamation, comes tangibly in communion, and goes with us as we are sent out as the body of Christ into the world. Everything about the Christian life is grounded in the truth that God has come into our midst in Jesus.

The incarnation reminds us that when God works, God does so in particular ways. God enters the context and becomes one with God's people. A key to understanding congregations is remembering that there are no generic people of God apart from actual people of God. The church is not just a concept to be understood. The church is a concrete expression of Christ in a particular place and time.

Article VII of the Augsburg Confession recognizes this as well. After defining church as the "assembly of all believers," it immediately takes the context seriously. And so it says that "it is enough for the true unity of the church to agree concerning the teaching of the gospel and the administration of the sacraments. It is not necessary that human traditions, rites, or ceremonies instituted by human beings be alike everywhere" (*The Book of Concord*, p. 43).

> **The church is a concrete expression of Christ in a particular place and time.**

The gospel brings with it God's commitment to take every place seriously enough to customize the way the work gets done. Congregations make the gospel come alive and show what God's kingdom looks like in that place. Engaging evangelism means speaking the gospel and inviting people into the community of God's grace.

When a congregation takes the incarnation seriously, its ministry becomes contextual and relevant in ways that allow the church to be Christ's voice and hands in the world. This means that teaching, preaching, worshiping, and cultivating relationships reflect the context in which the congregation is found and do so from the perspective of the gospel. While the church Don and Phyllis left often appeared out of touch and irrelevant, God is raising up new communities committed to contextual ministry.

This means that while congregations are a people set apart by God, they are also called to stay intimately connected and in relationship with that world. Martin Luther's commitment to get Scripture into the language of the people and his German mass were a result of his recognition that for the majority of people, the gospel needs to be accessible and culturally connected in order to be heard clearly. Jesus prayed for his followers during the last night of his life saying, "They do not belong to the world, just as I do not belong to the world. Sanctify them in the truth; your word is truth. As you have sent me into the world, so I have sent them into the world" (John 17:16-18). It seems that living in the tension between being contextual and set apart is what he had in mind.

God Sends Us into the World

The bridge between this purposeful and set apart church and the world to which it is sent is the people. A healthy congregation claims its identity as a community of ministers. The old model of a church as a building with a pastor who functions as the only minister won't work in this new setting. (It wasn't such a hot model before—we just were able to get away with it.)

A healthy congregation claims its identity as a community of ministers.

Congregational life is more like a seminary designed for laity, where people "practice" their faith, and learn from and grow with each other. The word *pastor* is used only once in Scripture, and the role is "equipping the saints" (Ephesians 4:11-12). Pastors are not chaplains but serve as trainers and coaches for a community of ministers, many of whom will be beginners. Those who belong to Christ gather for worship and nurture, training and support. They learn to teach and preach, lead and pray, care and share, study, and serve. They "practice" these things within the congregation. And then they are sent back into the world. This community of ministers (and remember, there will be some beginners!) needs to be equipped to live in the midst of the world in ways that speak, pray, and act as agents of the gospel.

Luther understood that all Christians are anointed as priests in baptism. Texts such as 1 Peter 2:4-10 and Revelation 1:5-6 helped him see this reality. Writing about this he said, "This is the true priesthood. As we have heard, it embraces these three things: to offer spiritual sacrifices, to pray for the congregation, and to preach" (*Luther's Works*, volume 30, *The Catholic Epistles*, Saint Louis: Concordia, 1967, p. 55). Imagine a congregation where all members see their lives as ministries lived out in the world and where their vocation is grounded in proclamation, prayer, and sacrificial service.

• *Proclamation:* God uses the church to provide the training needed to be effective at telling the story of Jesus in the world. Missionaries to the culture need practice telling it in the church so they will be confident telling it out in their world. Today only about half of Americans belong to a congregation, and on most Sundays at least five out of six Americans (a conservative estimate in my opinion) are not in worship. If most people are to hear about Jesus, it will not be from pastors speaking from the pulpits. It will be from each of us speaking in daily life.

• *Intercessory prayer:* Much of the rhetoric about the priesthood of all believers has been co-opted in the larger culture like this: "I don't need to go to church. I can talk to God for myself." But when the sixteenth-century reformers emphasized the right of all the baptized to approach God, it was tied to the responsibility to pray on behalf of others. The gift of prayer is an expression of love for our neighbor. Whoever gets to tell Don and Phyllis about what Jesus is doing will be praying for them. Prayer keeps a missionary people clear that they are about God's work and not their own.

• *Sacrifice:* Equipping God's people as priests will involve equipping people for service that includes the willingness to sacrifice for others. The age of comfortable Christianity is drawing to a close. This means deepening faith and strengthening character so that those sent out from our congregations are able to foster lifestyles of integrity that exhibit a sacrificial love of the neighbor. To be taken seriously when they speak, Christians will have to exhibit an almost counter-cultural commitment to live in new ways. Making difficult choices and speaking out even when there is a price to be paid will be essential. If Christians are just like everybody else and nobody else is a Christian, why bother?

God's new people can no longer see themselves as engineers, plumbers, and students who attend church. They must now see themselves transformed into a kingdom of priests, called to minister in the name of Jesus, and sent to infiltrate the world through their vocations as they work as engineers, plumbers, and students.

Summary

It is a strange new day to be the church. But God is up to something here! God is serious about conversion and is challenging the church today to *expect* lives to be changed by the good news of Jesus. God has called the church to be a people set apart, living a life that is different from the rest of the world. God has a dream for the church, that it will be completely caught up in God's special mission. God really cares about every place and challenges the church to do the same. And God is sending every single one of us into the world, which means the church needs to be about making sure every single one of us is trained and equipped for mission and ministry.

We Lutherans have remarkable theology for reaching people like Don and Phyllis. While they and tens of millions of others have stopped coming to us, we can finally practice what we have preached all along. We are a missionary people who are sent out by a missionary God to tell the story of Jesus, pray for those we encounter, and live sacrificial, cross-centered lives for the sake of the world. It may be that the world has stopped coming to us. But it is clear that God uses congregations to select, shape, and send us out in mission to the world—and we are almost everywhere!

For Reflection and Discussion

1. God is calling our congregations to get serious about conversion . . . about EXPECTING people's lives to be changed. Is this something YOUR congregation expects? What expectations does your congregation have for those who are "members"? What opportunities does your congregation offer to help people move from unbelief to disciple? How does your congregation encourage people to tell the story of how Christ has changed their lives?

2. What do you think God's purpose for your congregation is? If you aren't sure, how will you begin to work with others to discern it?

3. How does your congregation's life together (worship, teaching, group activities, and so on) build connections to the context to which God is sending you?

4. How many "ministers" are there in your congregation? How does your congregation set people free to see themselves as "priests"?

5. What strategy does your congregation have for equipping people to do the following?

> • Tell the story of Jesus in their daily lives.
>
> • Pray for the people they encounter.
>
> • Live cross-centered and sacrificial lives.

How can your your congregation do these things more effectively?

CHAPTER 5

What Is God up to in Our Communities?

Kelly A. Fryer

Who I Am in Christ . . .

I've been a pastor for almost 15 years, and right now I'm teaching at Luther Seminary in St. Paul, Minnesota. But the truth is, God and I have had a pretty rocky relationship over the years. Even after my heart finally melted and I turned to follow, I still find myself wrestling an awful lot. God has this weird habit of asking us to go places we really don't want to go. And I can be awfully stubborn.

But I keep following . . . because, when you come right down to it, where else is there to go? Jesus has the words of eternal life, right? He is the bread that fills up the emptiest, hungriest places inside of me. He is living water. And the fact that he ever bothered to show up, down here, right in the middle of my messy life, is still amazing to me. That's a gift I just can't seem to keep to myself.

One of the choir teachers at our local high school enthusiastically challenged this year's freshman class to come in with open minds, ready and eager to learn new things. "Avoid the dangers of tunnel vision," he exclaimed! He asked them to use "funnel vision" instead! Like "tunnel vision," "funnel vision" eventually gets pretty focused, which is important if you ever want to actually get anything done. But, unlike tunnel vision, "funnel vision" starts with a BIG vision, open wide at the top to all kinds of new experiences and ideas.

This is a pretty helpful image to use as we begin to think about what it looks like for a congregation to be engaged in God's central mission — engaging evangelism! — within the context of its local community.

God is at work in the world, creating and sustaining life, feeding the poor, healing the sick, forgiving sins, and setting people free. This is the big mission that all people are called to be a part of. Those of us who have answered the call to follow Jesus are also part of God's special mission of evangelism, living, and telling the story of Jesus that is good news for the world. But in order for us to actually get anything done, we need to have funnel vision. We need to focus our efforts carefully and thoughtfully, to make us as effective as possible within the particular mission field in which God has placed us.

Having funnel vision within our congregations begins with asking some important questions: Who lives in this community? What are their lives like? What questions are they asking? What needs do they have? What is important to them? How do they relate to one another? Who are the "invisible" people, the ones who live as outcasts and in the margins of the community? What beliefs do people in this community have about God? About church? What motivates them? Worries them? Brings them joy?

The truth is, our missionary God cares about the place where you live.

Using the answers to these and related questions, we can really focus our efforts and carefully steward our resources in the work God has called us to do. As a matter of efficiency and effectiveness, our congregations need to pay attention to the historical, geographical, cultural, and structural context within which they are located. It just makes good sense. And there are all kinds of resources to help congregations do that today.

But, more than pragmatic concerns are at stake here. The truth is, our missionary God *cares* about the place where you live. God loves the people who live in your neighborhood and will stop at nothing to get through to them with that good news. That is why God pays such careful attention to all of the things that make your particular community unique . . . and wants you and your congregation to do the same.

In fact, God is already at work in your community, in and through the people who live there. In some ways, our job as the church is simply to recognize and catch up with what God is already doing!

So . . .what IS God up to in our communities?

God Is Using Us to Change Our Communities

The congregation that I was a part of on September 11, 2001, celebrated the grand opening of its new ministry center just two days before those horrific events exploded onto our TV screens and into our national imagination. The congregation had just finished an eight-year process of redevelopment and relocation, during which time we worshiped in a variety of locations around the community, including a small storefront that had previously been used as a convenience store. After we moved out, a Middle Eastern store and restaurant moved in.

We were, of course, as shocked and angry as anyone by what happened in New York City, in the middle of Pennsylvania, and at the Pentagon that day. We mobilized for prayer and whatever practical help we could offer. We believed that our new doors had opened just in time and we did whatever we could to be a source of comfort, hope, and reassurance during what was, in many ways, the scariest time any of us had ever faced.

But we were just as shocked and angry by what happened here in our own community in the aftermath of those awful events.

That Middle Eastern grocery store—the one operating in a place that had for several years been our *church*—became the target of someone's hateful rage. The windows of the place were smashed in and horrible things were spray painted across its walls. Understandably, the owners felt threatened by these actions. In fact, we all felt a little threatened by these things. Suddenly, violence was a reality in our own backyard. And no place—no one—was safe.

Within an hour, members of the congregation were on the scene, offering to clean up the mess and assuring our frightened friends that they were not alone. They did this knowing that, by extending friendship and help to these Middle Eastern neighbors, they themselves might become targets of violence. They didn't think it was likely. But it didn't matter. Their sense of outrage and need to do the right thing far outweighed any fear they might have felt. The following weekend, about half of the congregation showed up for lunch after worship . . . even those whose taste buds would have preferred a hamburger to hummus any other day.

We live in a broken world. Sin seeps into every conversation and every relationship, every thought and every action, every private home and every public institution. Sometimes it explodes, and we find ourselves suddenly in the middle of divorce court or on a battlefield in a faraway land. Martin Luther explained it the only way he knew how. He said the devil was loose in the land ("The Large Catechism," *The Book of Concord,* p. 448):

> . . . like a furious foe, he raves and rages with all his power and might, marshaling all his subjects and even enlisting the world and our own flesh as his allies. For our flesh is in itself vile and inclined to evil, even when we have accepted God's Word and believe it. The world, too, is perverse and wicked. Here the devil stirs things up, feeding and fanning the flames, in order to impede us, put us to flight, cut us down, and bring us once again under his power.

No wonder Paul described the whole world as "groaning," waiting to be rescued once and for all from the powers of sin and death (Romans 8:19-23). I know I feel that way a lot. I bet you do, too.

Now, of course, we know that a rescuer *has* come. His name is Jesus. And, with his coming, God announced to the world that things were never going to be the same again. "The time is fulfilled!" Jesus declared, "and the kingdom of God has come near!" (See Mark 1:15.) Jesus came to heal the sick and chase away demons and set people free. In him, God came busting through the darkness to save the world from the enemy and from our own worst selves. God became one of us! God changed history forever. Now, because of Jesus, we know how this story ends: The good guys win! Even the bad guys get turned around. Because of Jesus, we know beyond any doubt that, one day, everything wrong will be made right.

And, in the meantime — get this! — God sends us.

When people look at us, they should know that God is up to something!

You and I (and our congregations) are the bridge between God's declaration that, in Jesus, the kingdom has come near, and that last day, when the kingdom comes in all its fullness. It is our job, in this *in-between time,* to be a sign of that kingdom. When people look at us, they should know that God is up to something! They should be able to catch a glimpse of what God's kingdom looks like. They should hear in our words a message of hope and promise and peace and justice and everlasting joy. They should hear the very voice of God, calling them to follow Jesus into new life.

God is using *us* to change the world . . . and that happens every time we sweep up broken glass . . . and make friends out of enemies . . . and welcome strangers . . . and do the right thing even when it is scary or dangerous . . . and keep our promises . . . and name the name of Jesus . . . and give ourselves away.

This Means We Have to Speak Their Language

God is using *us* to change the world. And this starts with the people in our neighborhoods. It begins right here, among the people in the communities where our congregations have been planted. This means we are going to have to be able to speak their language. And that means we are going to have to get to know them.

It is a terrible thing when congregations try to do ministry without getting to know their neighbors or without paying attention to how best to communicate with them. I don't think we mean to do this. We just forget that not everybody knows what we're talking about. They don't understand our customs. They don't know our story. And so we just go about our business, "doing church" like we've always done it, without realizing that what we're doing might not make any sense to our neighbors. This happens all the time. And the congregations I have been a part of have been as guilty of this as anybody.

One Palm Sunday morning about 10 years ago, for example, I watched as a young family walked through the doors of our church for the first time. I was so happy to see them. We had met the week before while I was out visiting in the neighborhood, inviting people to Holy Week and Easter worship. The mom, dad, and three little kids made their way all the way up the aisle to the front row; the only seats left. The children had never been to church before. It had been decades since mom and dad had bothered. Consequently, none of them really knew what to do.

The kids were wacky, pulling on their mom and dad, and wiggling around all through worship. The dad did his best to keep them under control and at least pretend to participate. It was hard. There was the green hymnal and another songbook to page through, and a bulletin with about a dozen flyers stuck in the middle of it. Too many papers. Too many page numbers. Too much work. The dad was obviously growing increasingly frustrated, but the last straw came when one of the children bumped into him as he stood trying to find something in the hymnal. Everything in his hands went flying. Papers everywhere. He closed the book, picked up the papers, put everything down, and folded his arms across his chest. He was done. He didn't sing or pray or participate again from that moment on. When they left the church that day, it was the last time I ever saw them.

That was the first time it really hit me that so much of what we do in our congregations is foreign to people who aren't used to going to church. We have our own secret language that includes funny words no one else in the world ever uses, words like *gospel* and *justified*. We have our own way of dressing (or at least the pastor does) that doesn't look like anything you'd see people wearing in everyday life. We have our own music, which sounds so very old-fashioned, especially when it's played on an organ. (Who listens to organ music on the radio?!?) We even have our own strange numbering system (well, *Lutheran Book of Worship* does, anyway). The whole experience seems *designed* to make strangers feel like they don't belong.

Again, I don't think we *mean* for it to be this way. But if God is going to be able to use us to make a difference in our communities, we really need to be willing to learn . . . and *use* the local language. Let's face it, even God found it necessary to figure out how to speak to us in a way that would make sense! The Bible tells us, "The Word became flesh and lived among us" (John 1:14). God could have just spoken the Word in some kind of divine, heavenly language; instead, *God became a human being* so that we could really hear and understand the Word. God, in Jesus, didn't just get to know us; God became one of us.

> **God, in Jesus, didn't just "get to know" us; God became one of us.**

Frankly, nothing should be more important to us, as Lutherans, than sharing the good news about God's love through Jesus in a way that people can understand. The Augsburg Confession, a document that has shaped Lutheranism for 500 years, defines the church as "the assembly of saints in which the gospel is taught purely and the sacraments are administered rightly" (The Augsburg Confession, Article VII, "Concerning the Church," *The Book of Concord*, p. 43).

Well, this doesn't mean just making sure our doctrine is correct. It doesn't mean having fancy sermons delivered by professionals with big voices (who are also well trained in how to stand just right at the altar, hands perfectly positioned at "2" and "10"). The gospel is taught, and the sacraments are administered "rightly" ONLY when they are shared in a way that makes sense to people. Our congregations are responsible for making sure they are communicating the good news about Jesus in a way that people can actually understand.

The sixteenth-century German reformers—who got Lutheranism started—did everything they could think of to help people understand the good news. They translated the worship service—and the Bible!—from Latin (which only the priests and scholars understood) into German (the language that most people there DID speak). The reformers used tunes from secular songs everybody knew to write songs about God. Martin Luther even wrote a simple book, the Small Catechism, to help parents teach their children about the faith. These guys—who got our church started—paid attention to the people who lived in their community and tried to speak their language. Our job today is exactly the same thing.

This Means We Have to Get to Know Them

Speaking the language of people in our communities begins, of course, with getting to know them. So, how exactly do we get to know our neighbors? How do we "read" our context? Well, there is probably no better way to start than with the way the apostle Paul did it. He got to know a community by . . . walking around.

There is a great story in the Bible about Paul and his visit to the city of Athens. When he got there, he had a little time on his hands. He was waiting for his friends Silas and Timothy, whom he had left behind in his rush to get out of the city of Beroea because his preaching had started a riot there! And, while he waited, "he was deeply distressed to see that the city was full of idols" (Acts 17:16).

Now, the people of Athens loved to listen to philosophers and religious people and pretty much anyone who had anything interesting to say. (This was entertainment in the days before *Mario Brothers* and TiVo.) So they brought Paul into the center of town and asked him to give a speech, which he did.

Paul stood up before them and said, "Athenians, I see how extremely religious you are in every way. For as I went through the city and looked carefully at the objects of your worship, I found among them an altar with the inscription, 'To an unknown god'" (Acts 17:22-23).

You can just see Paul, can't you? Wandering around the city. Making his way through the marketplace. Stopping at the local diner for a cup of coffee and a donut. Thumbing through the local newspaper. Listening in on conversations people were having on the street corners. Talking to the locals. Getting to know people. Finding out what was important to them . . . what they were worried about . . . what they felt passionate about . . . what their lives were like. *Caring* about them. Honoring them.

"I see how extremely religious you are!" he said, recognizing right away what was good and admirable about them. "But listen," he continued,

What right do we have to evangelize people who already have some kind of faith?

This is a good question. The answer is, if our faith in Jesus Christ has made a difference in our lives, what right do we have NOT to share it?!? We can tell the story in a way that is respectful of others and honors their faith, but we cannot keep the story to ourselves. It is just too good not to share!

"I want you to know something. This 'unknown god' of yours has a name. And his name is Jesus!" (Read Acts 17:16-33 to get the whole story.)

Paul wouldn't have known what these people needed to hear unless he spent time getting to know them. And he did that by walking around. This is still a pretty good way of getting to know people in a community.

A lot of congregations find it helpful and necessary to be intentional about this, though. They spend time going out in teams of two, knocking on doors, asking people in the community a few simple questions:

- What do you like most about this community?

- What do you think the biggest needs are in this community?

- What could a church do to be helpful to the people in this community?

Nothing beats this kind of direct contact with people in the community to help a congregation really get to know what their neighbors are thinking and needing and hoping for.

Many congregational leaders, though, also want to have some hard numbers to help them understand their context. They can go on-line, right to the U.S. Census Bureau to look up by zip code the most recent information about who lives in their particular community. It is possible to find all kinds of information about the gender, age, race, income level, and so on of people in a local community this way. Sometimes churches are surprised to find that their membership is not necessarily reflective of the communities where they are located. Our congregations are often more wealthy . . . and more white . . . than the people in our neighborhoods. Looking at the numbers can help us ask ourselves some very important and hard questions.

God is using us to make a difference in the lives of the people who live in our communities. But we can't do that very effectively if we don't speak their language! And we can't speak their language unless we get to know them.

God Is Using Our Communities to Change Us

God is using us to change our communities. That's one of the things God is up to! But, rest assured, God is also using *our communities* to change us.

That poor dad, who sat out most of Palm Sunday, had a greater impact on that congregation than he ever knew. Worship was never the same after that day. Today, everything a person needs to participate in the worship service is up in front, on a screen. And that's just for starters. Sometimes, on that screen, there are movie clips to help illustrate the sermon or a song. And the music? The message is all about Jesus, but the music sounds like the stuff people in that community listen to on their radios.

If we are really serious about doing ministry within the context, we have been placed in and developing any kind of meaningful relation-ship with our neighbors, then we should be prepared to be changed. These changes will be stylistic. But they will be more than that, too. When we really engage our community, even the *substance* of what we do and who we are will change. We don't have to look any further than the Bible to see how this works!

In the beginning of the church, in the very earliest days after Jesus left the apostles in charge, everybody just sort of assumed that the community of faith would only include Jewish people. Jesus was

Jewish. All of the disciples were Jewish. Their friends were all Jewish.
The Jewish community was the only community they had ever known.
It just made sense. But then, one day, the Spirit of God led
Peter—the head honcho of the church back then—to the home
of a man who was NOT as Jewish as you could be.

We should be prepared to be changed.

Cornelius was a Roman soldier, a member of the Italian guard.
He was a good man who loved God. One day, while praying as
he usually did, Cornelius heard God tell him to invite Peter
over to his house. So he did. And Peter came.

"Now," Cornelius said, "all of us are here in the presence of God to
listen to all that the Lord has commanded you to say" (Acts 10:33).
Cornelius thought that he had something to learn from Peter—that
through Peter, his life would be changed. It was. Cornelius and his
whole household were baptized that day, in the name of the Lord
Jesus. But Cornelius wasn't the only one changed. Peter was, too.
And through Peter, the whole history of Christianity changed course.

"I truly understand," Peter said to Cornelius, "that God shows no
partiality, but in every nation anyone who fears him and does what
is right is acceptable to him" (Acts 10:34-35).

In other words, Peter said, Jesus isn't just for Jewish people. Jesus is
for ALL people. From that day forward, the Christian church was intentional about taking its message about Jesus to everyone. This meant
all kinds of changes for the Christian community. Some of them were
stylistic. When they went to write down the story of Jesus, for example,
in the books of the New Testament, they did it in *Greek* instead of in
Hebrew or a Jewish dialect, which the disciples actually spoke. They
used Greek because that is the language the whole non-Jewish world
used back then.

But the changes in the church, after Cornelius, were substantive, too.
The Christian community changed their ideas about what kinds of food
you could eat (you could eat anything from now on!). They changed
their entrance requirements for becoming part of the community

(no more circumcision required!). They changed the direction of their mission (up and out, throughout the whole Roman Empire, and not just inward toward Jerusalem and Judea). As those early Christians engaged their context, the people in their communities were changed. But, just as surely, those early Christians were changed, too.

The truth is, God was already at work in their communities. God was at work in people like Cornelius. And God used those people to change the church.

Are our churches today ready and open to being changed by the communities they serve? As Lutherans, we ought to be. We know that there is only one thing that really matters . . . getting out the good news about the God we know in Jesus, a God who comes down here to save us and to set us free, a God who calls us out of an old life of death and darkness and into a new life of service and witness. All of our customs, traditions, ceremonies, worship practices, and so on are matters of "indifference," and "the community of God in every place and at every time has the authority to alter such ceremonies according to its situation, as may be most useful and edifying for the community of God" ("Concerning Ecclesiastical Practices," Formula of Concord, Epitome, Article X, *The Book of Concord*, p. 515).

> **There is a lot wrong with our communities. But God is at work out there, too.**

Maybe if we were absolutely clear about what really DOES matter, we would be open to the things we could learn from people in our communities. And, as Cornelius and Peter would tell us, people out there have a lot to teach us.

The world we live in is broken. And there is a lot wrong with our communities. But God is *at work* out there, too, in our neighborhoods and in the people who live in our communities. God is opening up hearts and minds, leading people into acts of mercy and kindness, breaking down barriers between people of different backgrounds, moving people to care for the environment. There are things we can learn from people out there. There are aspects of the culture that we can use as we do our job as God's people in this world. God wants to use our communities to change *us*.

Summary

Each one of us—and each of our congregations—is called to participate in God's special mission. Our job, as the church, in this *in-between time*, is to be a kind of bridge between the radical announcement that the kingdom has come near in Jesus . . . and the day when that kingdom finally comes in all its fullness. And we do this within the context of our local neighborhoods and our particular communities. God wants to use us to change our communities. Engaging evangelism means getting to know the people and learning to speak their language. But be prepared; God will also change *us* in that encounter!

For Reflection and Discussion

1. Think about the history of your community. How has it changed over time in terms of culture, race, economics, and so on?

2. Think about the history of your congregation. How has it changed over time in order to do a better job of sharing the good news about Jesus with people in the community?

3. How open do you think your congregation is to change right now? What makes you think that? What changes have recently been made to meet the needs of people in your community? What changes do you think still need to be made?

4. Has your congregation ever done a serious study of its context? How long ago? If a study has been done within the last five years, pull it out and use it to evaluate how well-prepared you are to share the good news in your community today. If the study is older than that (or you've never done one), find a resource to help you do a new study. (Try using, for example, *Our Context: Exploring Our Congregation and Community,* Augsburg Fortress, 2002.)

Sharing the Story

PART TWO

CHAPTER 6

Building a Missional Congregation

Michael W. Foss

Who I Am in Christ . . .

I am a pastor at Prince of Peace Lutheran Church in Burnsville, Minnesota. I have great confidence in the Holy Spirit to work within and through God's people for the sake of Christ in our world.

God is on a mission in this world. And our congregations are invited to be a part of it. In fact, unless we are a part of God's central mission—engaging evangelism—we are not the church at all! But how? How do you build a missional congregation that shares the story? This is a critical question for Christians today who believe that God is calling us to be partners in changing the world. So, let's begin Part Two here, with five keys to building a missional congregation: share the mission, help people tell the story, celebrate the community, expect people to experience grace, and practice what we preach.

Share the Mission

"When God made mud pies," I said, "Newfoundland was one of God's best." Our guide and new friend simply smiled. We had met two nights before when my brother and I arrived at our base camp. That evening he learned that I was a pastor—and that led to conversation about faith. If our guide had any, it was deeply personal and private. He didn't attend church. Later I would learn that his wife had been part of an abusive Christian sect. Her experience had soured them both on the institutional church with its rigid set of doctrines and hierarchy of power. God was a possibility . . . but church was not. So, when we were out hiking in the beauty of the Newfoundland wilderness, I couldn't help but share my gratitude for just being there. Our guide, I believed, could connect the wonder of the land he loved with Creator God. If he could hear a word from me that was grace filled, if he could catch sight of a faith that didn't make excessive demands but accepted him for who he was, then maybe the Holy Spirit could begin the creative process of faith building.

There are three great creations of God. The first was the forming of the universe itself. As Christians, we believe that the love of God overflowed the boundaries of eternity and took shape in the physical creation around us. My reference to God making mud pies was a bit whimsical, I admit. But the metaphor works for me because I believe God delighted in the making of creation—not unlike a child delights in the making of mud pies! In any case, God's love took shape in the making of our world and God's delight is expressed in the first chapter of Genesis by the repetition of this phrase: ". . . and God saw that it was good." And, finally, "God saw everything that he had made, and indeed, it was *very good*" (Genesis 1:31, italics added).

The second great creation of God's love was the creation of God's people, Israel. In Genesis 12, God creates faith in the call of Abram and Sarai. The point was to empower people with a witness to the truth of the character of God. This is ultimately expressed in the language of God's call to the people of God at Sinai: "Now therefore, if you obey my voice and keep my covenant, you shall be my treasured possession out of all the peoples. Indeed, the whole earth is mine, *but you shall be for me a priestly kingdom and a holy nation*" (Exodus 19:5-6, italics added). God chooses to partner with people in order to become known in the world. Surely we must understand that a priestly people does not exist for itself, but is consecrated to serve on behalf of God for the sake of others. Israel, as God's second great creation, was a people made for witness and created for mission—the mission of making God known to a world beset by a pantheon of gods who were not gods at all.

The third great creation of God is the Christian church. We are God's *new* missional people. God's love would not be limited by the boundaries of eternity—so God created. And God's love would burst through the hidden limitations of creation and call forth a witnessing people, Israel. Finally, God's love would shrug off the ethnic parameters of Judaism and form a missional people from every tribe and nation of the world. This is the Christian church. Mission and witness are not what we do; they are part and parcel of who we are. Jesus articulated this mission—"All authority in heaven and on earth has been given to me. Go therefore and make disciples of all nations" (Matthew 28:18-19). The Holy Spirit is given to empower us for the mission—"You will receive power when the Holy Spirit has come upon you; and you will be my witnesses in Jerusalem, in all Judea and Samaria, and to the ends of the earth" (Acts 1:8).

> *We are a people of grace who have a story to tell.*

Through three great creations, God has extended an invitation of grace: Be my partners in caring for creation and humankind through word and deed. We are people created by the unexpected and unearned love of our Creator in Jesus Christ. We are a people of grace who have a story to tell. Our witness is to the God of grace revealed in Jesus of Nazareth. Our mission is to make known throughout the world the truth that God desires an eternal relationship with every person. That was *my* mission as I hiked through the Newfoundland wilderness with our guide. This is *our* mission, together. Missional congregations are formed as we grow in understanding that we share this mission.

Help Each Other Tell the Story

"I don't have a faith story," she said. When Brianna was asked to share her faith story as part of one of our confirmation services, this was her response. "After all," she continued, "I've been a Christian all my life." But later, she reflected on the opportunity and said, "I have been a believer all my life, but through the ministry of this church I have discovered a deep and personal relationship with Jesus Christ that I never had before. I love this church!"

Each Christian has a faith story. Some may be dramatic. Others are not—like Brianna's. But the activity of the Holy Spirit in our lives to produce and grow faith is very real. One of the great tasks of the church is to help people get in touch with their faith stories, to help them articulate the ways in which their lives have been transformed by God's activity in their lives.

There are three key components of this task. The first is to affirm God's deep desire to be in personal relationship with every person. This theological witness creates an open door for conversation that begins with the question "How has God been active in your life?" This simple question does two things. It gently asserts an essential element of our faith— that God is active in every life of faith. And it invites personal reflection on the active presence of God for that person. This reflection is the basis for discovering our faith story. For Brianna, the invitation to share her story pushed her to reflect on how God had been active in her life and where the church fit in.

Authenticity, not perfection, is the goal of sharing.

The second key component is to provide an initial non-threatening context in which the person can reflect, share, and refine their story. This is often done in conversation with a trusted friend or Christian leader. A teen staff member was the trusted friend who listened to Brianna and helped her get in touch with her story and refine it so that she would be willing to share it.

The third key component is to clearly state that authenticity, not perfection, is the goal of sharing. We have an incredible theology— if we would only live it! The Reformation principle that we are saints and sinners simultaneously makes it clear that perfection is not possible this side of eternity. Yet, we often have unintentionally given the impression that Christian witness must be perfect in order to be effective. A cursory glance at the lives of the disciples dispels this notion. Many people are hesitant to share about faith because their only models are negative. They can't get to a place of comfort with their inadequacies and imperfections in order to understand that their very vulnerability is what can be most compelling about their faith sharing. Brianna's honesty and authenticity was clear precisely because her sharing wasn't perfect—it was real. The invitation we have to share with the world is to a real faith in real life. Our witness is most effective when that is what we reflect.

Each one of us has a story. It is one of the primary tasks of the congregation to help us get in touch with that story. But let's be clear: This story is for telling. While the faith we share is an intensely personal thing, it is never a private matter. Sooner or later, the activity of God in the life of an individual will turn that person outward in witness—whether through sharing in words or in deeds of kindness and justice. The invitation to partner with God is an incredible affirmation of our value. But it is not ours to claim for ourselves alone. And missional congregations emerge as people are encouraged to tell their stories.

Celebrate the Community

One of the reasons we are often tempted to keep our stories to ourselves is that, in our culture, we have confused the ethic of "rugged individualism" with the personal nature of faith. But there is nothing private about faith. And there is no clearer proof of that than the way God gathers us together, as one body, into local congregations . . . *public* institutions! . . . communities of strangers.

We have too often failed to boldly declare the power and necessity of the local congregation. Such thinking is simply not biblical. God always has called to faith and from faith into community. In the best-known Bible verse we read, "For God so loved *the world* that he gave his only Son" (John 3:16, italics added). It doesn't read that God so loved *the individual alone.* No one comes to faith without the witness of the community. And no one who comes to faith is left alone apart from community.

For example, the promise given to Abram and Sarai in Genesis 12:1-2 reads, "Now the Lord said to Abram, 'Go from you country and your kindred and your father's house to the land that I will show you. I will

make you *a great nation,* and I will bless you, and make your name
great, so that you will be a blessing'" (italics added). The promise is for
the blessing of community—a great nation. This promise is kept in the
forging of Israel. And it is fulfilled in Jesus, as he gathered together
twelve disciples whose first big act was to create that Christian community in Jerusalem and whose second big act was to extend that community throughout the world. In fact, the bulk of the New Testament is
either a description of the emergence of such communities in mission
(the book of Acts) or letters written to encourage and build up congregations of faith.

Now, I don't intend to say that congregations are Christ's exclusive
form for the church. But I do intend to say that they are the primary
form of his church. We need to reclaim this essential biblical teaching
and celebrate that God has gathered us into community! Why is it that,
statistically, a Lutheran Christian invites another person to church only
once every 27 years or so? I think it is because we have divorced our
faith from the essential of community worship. Witness without congregational worship rings hollow. Biblical faith is both personal and corporate. Brianna instinctively understood that. Her faith story was also a
witness to the power of the institutional church to change lives. Her
story was connected to the community.

The congregation is an indispensable part of God's mission and the task
of evangelism. First of all, this is the community that strengthens and
encourages us to tell the story. This is especially true today: We have
emerged into a pre-Christian era. By this I mean that our cultural context has moved out of an assumed Judeo-Christian ethic and into a
polytheistic one. This doesn't mean that we are no longer spiritual.
Nothing could be further from the truth. It means that there is no una-
nimity or core understanding of spirituality that predominates and
informs the world in which most of us live. The passive Christian, the
silent witness of faith, is no longer workable. Christians of every age
are beset by choices and alternatives that will push us to the core of
what we hold to be true. The congregation is one of the primary inter-
preters of what we truly believe. As long as our faith was unconsciously

supported in the past by our neighbors and the institutions of our society, the notion that faith changed lives was not necessary. But with the advent of our polytheistic world, such a belief is essential for a witnessing people. Otherwise, what is the point of evangelism? The congregation is where we are encouraged to share the faith that has transformed us.

Evangelism assumes that Jesus Christ changes lives.

Also, it is in the congregation that transformation itself occurs. One of the great tragedies of the late twentieth century was the loss of people's confidence in the power of the Holy Spirit to really change lives. Preachers preach, people worship and pray, grace is said at meal times — and the assumption has been that nothing changes. So we teach that, as a last resort, when all else fails . . . pray. Yet most of us have personally experienced the power of prayer to change things — and us! Many of us have seen the power of faith to change the lives of others and, yet, have forgotten its power to shape and change our lives. Evangelism assumes that Jesus Christ changes lives. Congregations in mission and witness can be bold when we trust that the Holy Spirit, as the author of faith, will work through us whether we see the outcomes desired or not.

Building a missional congregation happens as we celebrate that God has called and gathered us into a community where lives are changed and we are encouraged to tell the story to others.

Expect People to Experience Grace

The best evangelists are those whose lives have been touched by the grace of God and who are empowered by the Holy Spirit to share their stories. This is exactly what I have seen in my pastoral experience. The greatest advocates of faith have been those whose lives have been touched, blessed, healed, and strengthened in times of great personal need. When a spouse or child is lost, we have an incredible opportunity to reach out in Christ's name, not to provide answers, but to demonstrate and share the promise of forever. When an individual goes through a significant life transition (a divorce, the birth of a child, the sudden loss of a job, or retirement) the congregation has the possibility to reach out in Jesus' name. And when I have seen the local church do so, I have heard stories of faith spoken with gratitude and enormous power. This is not the intent of our care, but it can certainly be a great outcome!

"How does faith help you in your situation?" This is the usual way that my friend, a psychologist, introduces the spiritual into his professional care for others. He assumes that faith can be a vital ingredient in overcoming and growing through tragedy and loss. But he is respectful that not everyone has faith or the ability to access it. So, this is the shape of his question. And it has led to enormous breakthroughs in therapy.

Think about it. What are the necessary components for my friend to ask this question? First, he has experienced the power of faith to be "useful" in his own life—as he puts it. Next, he assumes that if it is useful to him that it could be useful for others as well. He then trusts that each person has equal access to the power of the spiritual. And, lastly, he believes that their accessing of faith will, in fact, change their lives.

This friend came to faith within his congregation. His faith experience has led him to quietly, respectfully introduce faith to his clients. They can choose to pursue that line of thought or not, based on their life histories and beliefs. But, without his confidence that faith changes things, I doubt he would bother introducing the topic. Missional congregations will expect people to experience God's grace within their community, confident that this experience will lead them to share their faith with others.

Practice What You Preach

How do we implement ministries of evangelism? How do we shape congregations so that faith stories can be developed and shared? Missional congregations have to practice what they preach. If they preach that Christ changes lives, then they have to be willing to change themselves.

First, I believe we need to change the fundamental goal of our ministries. We need to replace the membership model with a discipleship model. The membership model has served us well for decades, but its time has passed. When the membership model was most effective, people presumed that responsibilities came along with belonging. In today's world, however, membership is all about privilege. Our consumer mentality has changed the meaning of membership so that it is about what we get—not how we grow or what we give.

Let's be honest. If we really do all the things you're suggesting, some people in my congregation are going to get mad. What do we do about that?!?

Well, first of all, we need to stop being so afraid to disagree with one another. Look at the stories in the Bible, they are full of conflict! Think of Sarah and Hagar . . . David and Saul . . . the prophets and everybody! . . . Peter and Paul. A healthy congregation is NOT "conflict-free." (There really is no such thing, anyway—there is just HIDDEN conflict, which isn't good for anyone.) A healthy congregation is one where people are open about things and willing to engage one another in honest, helpful dialogue.

Second, as we are in conversation together we need to remind each other to love GOD—and God's mission in the world—even more than we love our CHURCH. This will help keep us focused on the most important thing as we try to make decisions about what to do and how to do it.

Third, there WILL be some people who just don't want to be a part of a congregation that is about MISSION first, who can't handle being in a congregation where people are involved in healthy debate, who just can't deal with change. They may decide to find another church home. Pray for them. Love them. But do not let them stop God's mission in your place. Send them off with your blessing, trusting that God is at work in their lives, too.

—*Kelly A. Fryer*

Discipleship radically changes the direction of our ministry. There is a great sense of privilege — of knowing God in Jesus Christ. But the focus is on following the Savior, of conforming our lives to his teaching and sharing our faith. Discipleship ministry strives to grow people deep in God with the clear understanding that such growth will necessarily turn them outward to the world. Then the task of the local congregation is to both call to faith and then equip the faithful with the spiritual tools to live that faith in an indifferent and skeptical world.

So, second, leaders must change. The focus on leadership is no longer to do the work of the ministry but to identify the gifts of disciples and equip *them* for the doing of ministry. Pastors cannot be the primary evangelists in the world. The people of God are the first-line missionaries. The truth of the matter is that people will be in conversations with others that pastors will never be invited into. They will have greater potential for being heard than the clergy will.

The people of God are the first-line missionaries.

I say this not to lessen the role of pastors or congregational staff, but to elevate and differentiate the roles of both staff and laity. Pastors and staff members are called to equip the laity for the witness of the church. This can happen through acts of service as well as the sharing of faith stories. A disciple understands that every act of kindness, every impulse for justice, will be accompanied by the name of the one through whom we have faith and for whom we live. Leaders are called to grow disciples. Disciples grow in relationship to their Master, Jesus. And the Savior brings with him a host of others that we are called to witness to and care for.

Third, preaching must change in order to include personal stories that affirm and testify to the fact that the gospel changes lives. The task of preaching has incredible power. God has staked God's word on it. Those of us who are responsible for delivering sermons in our congregations must understand that our preaching will set the stage, open the hearts and minds of our listeners, to the possibilities of God. I believe that every time I preach God can and will change someone's life. This may mean a change of perspective. It may mean that destructive behaviors cease or that a personal relationship can be healed or strengthened. Or, it may mean that someone will come to faith. These are the activities of the Holy Spirit—but the Holy Spirit works through the spoken word.

This expectation of preaching is affirmed and strengthened by the public sharing of those whose lives have been blessed and changed. What if the announcements in our worship service were not about the next women's tea (as important as that might be), but a time for someone to thank the congregation for their care or to share how God has changed their lives for the better? This can be as simple as Brianna's sharing, or it can be the witness of someone like the psychologist who has integrated faith into his professional activities. Such sharing will open the door of possibility for someone to think, "If he or she can do that, I can, too."

Furthermore, preachers and leaders will need to make the application and challenge of change clear for people. One of the ways I have discovered to do that is to introduce this question in a sermon: "What about you?" This question invites listeners to place themselves in the text. I may proceed by sharing suggestions for how a listener might implement the invitation to practice our faith contained in the text. Often I will speak specifically to teens or adults, to parents or children, to those single or widowed or divorced. These are always formed as suggestions that I try to respectfully set before my audience.

My experience is that most of the people in our churches want to live their faith but simply don't know how. When we talk about the practices of faith (prayer, Bible reading, Christian service, and giving) without sharing ways they might do them, our audience is no better off. Evangelical congregations strive to bridge the gap between what we say we believe and how we live. We do so by always speaking of God's grace and then by introducing ways each of us can practice our faith. There has been a consistent and strong affirmation of this preaching in our church. I have had the privilege of listening as disciples in congregations have spoken of the growing power of worship when the outcome we pray and work for is equipped lives.

Building a missional congregation means being willing to change even the most important things—like how leaders function and what preaching looks like—because God has chosen the Christian and the church to be partners in changing the world. My friend, Len Sweet, once said, "Christ doesn't call us to make a difference in the world but to make a different world!" (Prince of Peace conference, 1998). He's right! And the church really CAN do this. If that were not the case, I seriously doubt that the Berlin Wall would have been torn down. The activities of the Lutherans (and other Christians) to protest the grip of Communism can be directly tied to the groundswell that toppled not only a particular political system, but an entire world view!

Missional congregations are willing to change because they really believe they are God's partners in changing the world . . . beginning in their own contexts. They are not placed in their locations haphazardly. I believe that every church has a place and a particular task in the growing of God's kingdom. We can lose sight of this; we can lose heart and courage; and we will experience despair, decline and, eventually, death. But if we are open to this particular call of God, if we are willing to ask what God would have us do in our place and time, we can thrive and experience rebirth in our congregations. The key is the shape of the question.

Too often the question we ask is "What does the pastor or leader *think* we ought to do?" or "What do the people think we ought to do?" and not "What do we prayerfully discern is *God's will* for our ministries?" I do not intend to diminish the need for open conversation about these matters. What I do want to assert is that the common experience of individuals being guided by the Holy Spirit in their personal lives needs to be extended into the life of the congregation. If the Spirit of God leads individuals through prayer and the counsel of trusted friends, surely the Holy Spirit, given first to the gathered disciples on Pentecost, will guide the congregation that seeks to hear and follow.

Summary

The opportunities for the growth of Christ's church are enormous! But building a missional congregation will require a new confidence — confidence in our shared mission, confidence to tell the story, confidence in the importance and centrality of the congregation. And it will require a willingness to change our expectations and our behavior. Just as we preach that Christ changes individual lives, so too does Christ seek to change our communal life. Today, our congregations especially need to consider making big changes in our expectations of members, the role of leaders, and the function of preaching. Such changes are risky. But if we are willing to step out in faith, we will change the world in Jesus' name.

For Reflection and Discussion

1. How does it feel to think that God has invited you to be a partner in making God's love known in the world through Jesus Christ? Have you experienced God's leading in your life? In what ways? What does it mean for you to say that you are a part of God's mission?

2. How do you see the Holy Spirit leading and empowering the church for its mission? When was the last time your church prayed for God's leading in its mission? How are you a part of that?

3. Have you seen how faith has changed lives? What happened? How did it happen? What was (or could have been) the role of the congregation in it?

4. What changes does your congregation need to make in order to become a missional community? How willing is your congregation to make changes? How can you help move your congregation more fully into God's mission?

CHAPTER 7

Leading Congregational Transformation

Jeff Marian

Who I Am in Christ . . .

I grew up thinking that missionaries were people who preached the gospel in exotic places overseas. Gurnee, Illinois, is about 1,000 miles from the nearest sea, and it's anything but exotic, but that's my mission field. That's where I serve as pastor at Joy! Lutheran Church.

I have a passion for people who are lost on the treadmills of life, the treadmills of happiness or success or self-fulfillment. My heart aches for those who have been so beaten down in life that they can't imagine that the God of all creation loves them beyond reason. I hunger to share the good news with those who have not yet allowed their feet to walk the pathway of God's grace through Jesus Christ.

I'm wired this way because I've been one of those people. Grace has changed my life, and I still can't quite get over the fact that I've been given the privilege of telling others about that gift of God's grace.

In the United States, the church is planted in one of the world's largest mission fields. Jesus' words call to us with a new urgency, "The harvest is plentiful, but the laborers are few." I'm honored to be part of the harvest staff.

Our congregations are called to be a part of God's mission in this world. But how, exactly, does God go about building missional communities of faith? God uses ordinary people, of course! God calls out leaders like you and me to help transform congregations so that they can be God's instruments in the world, telling the story of Jesus to everyone, inviting them to be a part of God's mission, too. There are some very specific things that leaders can do in the work of congregational transformation. But transformational leaders never forget that, finally, this is God's work.

Transformational Leaders Know This Is God's Gig

Pastor Bob couldn't understand what was wrong. Before he'd taken the call to Grace Church four years ago, he had researched all the local demographics. The urban neighborhood where Grace was located was a growing and diverse garden of humanity. The call committee had been clear about their desire to reach out beyond Grace's walls. Within his first year, Bob had gathered the best leaders in the church and created an Evangelism Committee with clear roles and objectives. They'd even studied and implemented the latest evangelism program from a prominent mega-church. Despite all that, neither worship attendance nor membership had grown significantly in the past four years. What *was* growing was Bob's discouragement and doubt about his own leadership.

But transformational leaders never forget that, finally, this is God's work.

Pastor Sondra's cheeks were wet with tears. Those same cheeks also ached from excessive smiling. Just moments before, Sondra had baptized a family—a single father and two young children—into God's family, and now the father was giving a brief testimony to his new-found faith. Sondra wondered if she and the congregation would ever get used to hearing such stories, despite the fact they were becoming more and more commonplace at Faith Church. Sondra had to admit that she couldn't quite explain the transformation in this once stagnant church. The community's demographics were flat. The church's facilities weren't great. Faith Church didn't even have an Evangelism Committee. And yet Faith Church had nearly doubled its membership and more than doubled its worship attendance in the five years Pastor Sondra had been in leadership. Whether she was able to explain it or not, Pastor Sondra was thrilled to be along for the ride.

What made the difference? Leaders of both growing and declining congregations often have three things in common. First, they work hard. Second, they hunger to experience congregational growth in both depth and numbers. And third, they are hard-pressed to explain the results of their labors. Their struggle—the tension between the mystery of kingdom growth and our labors—is nothing new. It was well articulated by Jesus in the parable of the growing seed, "The kingdom of God is as if someone would scatter seed on the ground, and would sleep and rise night and day, and the seed would sprout and grow, he does not know how. The earth produces of itself, first the stalk, then the head, then the full grain in the head. But when the grain is ripe, at once he goes in with his sickle, because the harvest has come" (Mark 4:26-29). Like the farmer, we plant seeds, we sleep and rise night and day, and ultimately we are at a loss as to why the church grows or declines.

There is a necessary tension between the Holy Spirit's work and our labors, and there will always be a certain element of mystery as to why some churches grow while others do not, but the task of church leadership is not to explain growth or its absence. The task of church leadership is to discern what our labor is and then do that labor with joyful abandon, all the while recognizing the importance of the Holy Spirit's work. We cannot do the Holy Spirit's work and the Spirit will not do ours, but when both come together good things often grow.

So, what is the labor of the church in the fertile fields of God's world? For church leaders hungering to see their congregations grow, the answer begins with the transformation of congregational culture. While there will certainly be more work to be done when cultural transformation is completed, the journey must begin here. Any church leader who desires lasting change in the congregation will need to understand the basics of organizational culture and become skilled in the art of cultural transformation.

Transformational Leaders
Understand Organizational Culture

Every organization has a culture. An organization's culture is a shared set of values and beliefs that inform the way individuals and the organization as a whole perceive and react to their environment. Beliefs are those things an organization accepts as true. Values, which are often informed by beliefs, are the principles and behaviors that an organization holds to be of vital importance. Like the water that fish swim in, these beliefs and values are so much a part of the organization they are often taken for granted by the members. Leaders need to understand organizational culture because it drives behavior. It explains why members of the organization do what they do. If you scratch beneath the surface of congregational behavior, you will often uncover the beliefs and values of the organization.

The soil out of which engaging evangelism grows must be rich with the beliefs and values that support it.

While in seminary, I provided supply preaching for a congregation. I was nervous about the assignment, but my confidence grew as the service went along. By the end of the service, as I chanted the benediction, I was feeling pretty good. As the congregation sang the three-fold amen, I walked out of the sanctuary and waited in the narthex for the people to come filing out. But they didn't. They just sat there. And sat there. And sat there. Finally an usher came over to me and said, "Pastor, the service ain't over till you say, 'Go in peace, serve the Lord.'"

So, I walked back in and said the good words. With great relief and more than the usual gusto the people responded, "Thanks be to God!" Only then did the people get up and walk out.

That's organizational culture. Call it merely habit if you like, but the usher understood the truth: the congregation believed the service wasn't over until a certain set of words had been spoken, and that belief drove their behavior.

In any congregation, the soil out of which engaging evangelism grows must be rich with the beliefs and values that support it. I once met with a group of congregational leaders who were interested in evangelism. I challenged them to invite someone from their neighborhood to join them in worship within the next 30 days. When we got back together, one of the men in the group said he hadn't invited anyone because "everyone in my neighborhood already goes to church." When pressed on the issue, he shared his belief that everyone in the community was already active in a church. He had come to this conclusion because all the people he knew in his neighborhood (five families) already belonged to his congregation. He was shocked when he read the demographic data that said 55 percent of the people in his community were unchurched. His beliefs shaped his behavior. The next time we got together, he shared stories of having met new neighbors who were unchurched. He invited them to worship and one family actually attended!

Contrast that experience with this one told to me by a friend. Within six months of moving in, a new family organized a picnic in his neighborhood and provided all the food, beverages, and entertainment. It was the first event of its kind for this neighborhood. When the picnic was over, my friend, who happens to be a pastor, stayed to help clean up and asked this new family, "This was a great event. Whatever made you think of it?"

Their answer spoke volumes about their beliefs and values. They responded, "We're Christians and believe that it's important to share our faith with others, but we know sharing faith happens best through genuine friendships. This was our first step toward those friendships in this new neighborhood."

Transformational Leaders Close the Gap

Every congregation has a culture. Within that culture are certain beliefs and values held to be right and true. For many congregations, the idea of evangelism is one of those values. They say it's important. They believe that God has called their church to go and make disciples, but in reality new disciples are not being made. If values and beliefs drive organizational behavior, how can this be?

To answer this question it is helpful to distinguish between espoused and enacted values and beliefs. Espoused values and beliefs are those values and beliefs that are explicitly stated within the organization. They are the things we say we value and believe as a church. They might be printed out in a statement or taught in a new-member class. Enacted values and beliefs, on the other hand, are those values and beliefs that actually get translated into behavior within an organization. They are more than words. They are the foundation and motivation for actual behavior.

The reason this distinction is important is that it points to the fact that there is often a gap between espoused and enacted values and beliefs. What we say we believe and value does not always line up with what we actually do. I once served a congregation that espoused the value of being a welcoming congregation. One Sunday morning, a young woman came to worship. She had recently come out of a life of drugs and prostitution, and her journey toward wholeness brought her to church for the first time. She was hungry for a spiritual connection and for spiritual community. Unaware that the church had an unwritten dress code, this woman wore her everyday clothes, which were far more revealing than the clothing we usually saw on Sunday morning. It broke my heart to hear several members whisper behind her back about this "tramp" who was "a disgrace and offense to the Lord." The value of being a welcoming congregation was espoused, but not enacted.

Likewise, in an attempt to stoke an evangelism fire, many congregations have purchased and used programs that promise to transform them into a well-oiled evangelism machine. They recruit a committee. They study the materials. They might even offer a contemporary worship service so that their members can invite guests. But more often than not these congregations are sorely disappointed with the results. Their own members attend the contemporary service, but the guests just don't come. Why?

One Congregation's Story of Cultural Transformation

Shepherd of the Lakes Lutheran Church is located in Grayslake, Illinois, a far north suburb of Chicago. Founded in 1962, the congregation grew to about 180 people in worship by 1970 and stayed at that point. Pastor John Holm arrived in 1994 to serve the congregation. "The surrounding community had grown considerably in the 10 years before I arrived," Holm says, "but the congregation had not grown with it. . . . The people loved one another, and they loved the church, but they believed the church existed for them. They wanted guests to come, but they valued tradition so deeply they expected newcomers would become like them, and the church itself would not significantly change. In other words, they were looking for Lutherans who were just like them. Grayslake, however, was filled with people who didn't know a Lutheran from a lamppost."

Holm set upon the task of turning the congregation's culture inside out. He consistently upheld the mandate to go and make disciples, the call to the congregation to exist—not for itself—but for the thousands of people outside its walls who had no relationship with Jesus Christ. Holm reinforced these values in seminars, slogans, newsletters, and every venue he could find. As he says, "I cast the vision and held up the new beliefs and values so often I felt that if I said it just one more time, I'd be sick. But what I found was that the constant presentation was crucial to changing the congregation's mind-set."

As new behaviors began to surface, Holm honored them, reinforced them, harnessed the momentum, and built upon success. "I'm still meeting resistance," Holm says. "But the changes in this congregation have been so positive that resistance can't hold back the Spirit's momentum."

With a growing worship community of 525, today Shepherd of the Lakes is a congregation turned inside-out. This didn't happen with a program or an evangelism committee. It happened through cultural transformation. When the congregation's beliefs and values changed, so did its behavior.

Frequently, the problem lies in the gap between espoused and enacted values and beliefs. There's nothing wrong with evangelism programs. There are many excellent programs out there, but most of them seem to assume that the congregation's culture, values, and beliefs, support evangelism. That is a deadly assumption. Without a culture rich with espoused and enacted beliefs and values that support evangelism, most evangelism programs will fail to bring the promised harvest.

The gap between espoused and enacted beliefs and values is frequently a source of great frustration for congregational leaders. Although they exhort the members of the church to share their faith and invite people to worship, and preach and write about evangelism at least twice each year, evangelism just doesn't happen. This frustrating set of circumstances often causes church leaders to question their leadership or simply accept congregational decline as an unchangeable reality. The gap, however, between espoused and enacted beliefs and values can be narrowed and even closed. Congregational leaders who learn the art of cultural transformation become skilled in closing this gap and enjoy the rewards of a church that is behaviorally aligned with what it says is important.

Transformational Leaders Take Action

Walk the aisles of any bookstore and you'll discover dozens of volumes on organizational change. Walk the hallways of any corporation or congregation and you'll discover dozens of examples of failed change initiatives. We glibly say the only certainty in life is change, yet we tend to underestimate the challenge of deep, lasting organizational change. Since the majority of churches in America are either stagnant or declining, it is essential that church leaders help their congregations to boldly face the realities of their situation and cast a clear and compelling vision for change.

It is not the purpose of this chapter to lay out a complete blueprint for organizational change. This is only the beginning. For a complete look at organizational change, see John P. Kotter's book *Leading Change* (Boston: Harvard Business School Press, 1996). Kotter's eight steps to

You've convinced me! But, how can we get started? How can our congregation get clear about who we are and what we are being called to do?

Here's a suggestion to help you begin casting a compelling vision for change.

Gather a group of 12 to 15 key leaders (influencers) in your congregation for one or more brainstorming sessions. The goals of brainstorming are to 1) face your current reality without excuses, 2) develop a list of beliefs and values that will support evangelism in your context, and 3) develop a specific plan for embedding your agreed-upon values and beliefs within your congregation. Note: You might need six hours or more to effectively complete this work.

1. Come prepared with the congregation's membership and worship statistics for at least the past 10 years, if available. Start by reading Matthew 28:19-20 or Acts 1:6-8, and by spending time in prayer, asking for the Holy Spirit's help. Discuss the following questions, keeping good notes: What is engaging evangelism? What do we believe and value about evangelism? What do our membership and worship statistics say about what we really believe and value? How will our values, beliefs, and behaviors need to change if our circumstances are to change?

Keep the group focused on their own beliefs and behaviors. Don't accept easy answers or allow the conversation to drift into excuses. This is a time to squarely face reality.

2. Pray! Ask God to shape your congregation in accordance with God's hopes and dreams for you. Brainstorm a list of values and beliefs that you believe will support evangelism in your context.

3. Review your list of values and beliefs, then identify strategies for embedding them in the congregation. Next, develop a specific plan for embedding your beliefs and values. Be sure to include SMART goals in your plan (Specific, Measurable, Attainable, Reasonable, and Time-bound).

organizational change are clear and concise and provide a simple but effective process for lasting change. But don't be fooled by the simplicity of Kotter's steps. Deep organizational change is incredibly hard work. It takes focus, tenacity, and thick skin. Specific steps need to be taken in order for change to occur, and these steps must be walked with care and constant prayer. Here are several suggested action steps that transformational leaders can take to help close the gap and lead congregations into engaging evangelism.

Can I get that in writing?

Written statements of mission, values, and beliefs present a consistent picture of the preferred future to the members of the congregation. While many organizations have these statements, they are often hidden away in file cabinets and infrequently referenced. These statements should be before the congregation constantly, both verbally and in writing.

Preach it, sister—teach it, brother!

Both preaching and teaching are vital communication tools for casting vision, values, and beliefs. Wise preachers weave the congregation's espoused beliefs and values into every sermon and lesson. They do this both explicitly (specifically referencing their statements) and implicitly by using the power of stories which embody the espoused values and beliefs. Whenever possible, they tell the stories of their own members who are living out the values and beliefs which support evangelism. Many mission-minded preachers take time each year to preach a series of sermons on these beliefs and values. Perhaps the most important teaching opportunity for embedding a new culture is new member orientation. Wise evangelism leaders spend considerable time teaching new members the values and beliefs that mark their new church home, and don't hesitate to lay out specific behavioral expectations for these new brothers and sisters.

Ya gotta live it!

Leaders who fail to walk their talk soon lose their leadership. Instead, leaders must think deeply about the values and beliefs they espouse and live out the implications in their own lives. As a mission-driven pastor, one of the most important things I do to embed a missional culture is to tell the stories of people with whom I'm seeking to share the good news of God's love and grace through Jesus Christ. Pastors and leaders who are unwilling to invest into personal and team evangelism should not expect their members to act differently.

Can I get a witness?

Allowing congregational members to share a personal testimony in worship, or to witness to what God is doing in their lives, is one of the most underutilized resources in the mainline church. Considering the incredible power of story, that's a great loss to the church. A well-prepared witness to the experience of God's love and grace in Jesus Christ helps to give a new vocabulary to those who wonder what they would say if they ever took the opportunity to share their faith.

It's a bird, it's a plane—no, it's an evangelism hero!

Reinforcement is a vital strategy for any change initiative. Make local heroes out of those who risk sharing their faith with others at home, in the congregation, and in their world. When someone lives out the beliefs and values that support evangelism, make a big deal out of it. Point to it and say, "Yes, that's what it looks like!" In addition to preaching and teaching, such heroes can be recognized in newsletters and with hand-written thank you notes.

Just say, "No!"

Old habits die hard. That's especially true in churches with deeply embedded cultures. During a change initiative, be on the lookout for beliefs, values, and behaviors that reinforce old patterns and undermine the desired new culture. Gently but firmly confront these situations and seek to put people on a new path of thinking and behaving.

Give it up!

Remember that tension between our work and the Holy Spirit's work? Let that tension remind the leaders of your congregation to pray daily for guidance, discernment, and wisdom. Pray alone and pray as a team.

Open every church gathering with a prayer that weaves in your beliefs and values.

Transformational Leaders Don't Quit

So . . . how are you feeling? Overwhelmed? Exhilarated? Frustrated? Hopeful? Scared? All of the above? Good! Jesus once said that the harvest was plentiful but the laborers were few. Are you willing to be a laborer and help develop more laborers for the harvest? I hope so. Jesus promised to be with us, and if we'll take up his yoke we'll discover the burden is light.

Let me share a few more thoughts about cultural transformation:

- It isn't easy. Knowing that the work of cultural transformation in the congregation is arduous will help keep you from frustration along the way. Start praying now!

- It isn't safe. Leaders who seek to be change agents need to know they're going to encounter opposition! Anticipate resistance. Know up front that not everyone will agree with or even go along with the changes you are going to suggest. Don't let that deter you. Your greatest defense against resistance is to base your efforts in a compelling, biblically grounded vision for the congregation's future.

- It isn't quick. This chapter is not intended to be a quick-fix solution. Cultural transformation takes time. It is slow-cooker work, not a quick fry. This level of change requires persistence and patience.

- It isn't over. While cultural transformation is the foundation of congregational change, it is not the end. Your new vision, beliefs, and values will call you to examine issues of worship, hospitality, staffing, and even your physical space.

- It's so worth the effort. Go back to the beginning of this chapter and read the story about Pastor Sondra again. What would you be willing to sacrifice to be part of a ministry like that? There is nothing like knowing God is at work changing lives with the gospel before your eyes.

Summary: Pastor Bob and Grace Church Revisited

Worship was over and the narthex was buzzing with conversation. As Pastor Bob shook hands with people, he had to remind himself that this was the same Grace Church he had been called to eight years before.

The last four years had been more challenging than any he had previously experienced. He remembered all the time he and the leaders of Grace had spent clarifying their values and beliefs. He smiled as he thought about the fact that he had cast the new vision, values, and beliefs for Grace Church so often the congregation had given him a T-shirt with the statements printed on the back. He still winced when he thought about the people who had since left the congregation, some with anger and unkind words. He prayed they would find a spiritual home where they might catch a new vision for mission, ministry, and evangelism. Was it all worth it? Bob asked himself.

Pastor Bob was brought back to reality when Barbara, a new member at Grace, called his name. "Pastor Bob, I want you to meet Elizabeth. She's just moved into the community and now works in my office. I invited her to worship this morning, and here she is." Pastor Bob couldn't help but notice the glow on Barbara's face. It was more than the fact that Barbara had brought a guest. It was a reflection of the fact that Grace Church had helped draw Barbara herself closer to Jesus Christ.

"It's a pleasure to meet you," Pastor Bob said. "Welcome to Grace Church. I can't tell you how glad I am that you came this morning."

For Reflection and Discussion

1. Think about the most effective leaders you have known. What characteristics do they share? What makes them effective?

2. When it comes to evangelism, what espoused values does your congregation have? In other words, what does your congregation "say" about it? What are you actually "doing" about it? Is there a gap? If yes, why do you think this is so?

3. You are being called to lead your congregation into transformation. How does that make you feel? What do you think about that? What special gifts do you have to help you do it? What are you lacking? What do you need to pray for in order to follow God into this adventure?

4. Why do you think it might be worth to leading your congregation into transformation? What do you think the outcomes might be? What difference will it make? Who will it make a difference for?

CHAPTER 8

Sharing the Story Every Day

Kirk Livingston

Who I Am in Christ ...

My purpose in life is to see Jesus better—daily, from God's Word—so I can love my wife as Christ loved the church, and so I can model love, purity, and obedience to my family and God's people. I aim to draw friends, strangers, and working people toward Christ by praying, writing, teaching, and telling the truth in simple and winsome ways that encourage. I try to gently apply insight from God's truth to Christians, non-Christians, and the general culture. I also head Livingston Communication, Inc., a marketing communication firm in St. Paul, Minnesota.

My new business cards showed up the day I ate breakfast with a friend. Between the eggs and toast and coffee, he groaned over his disappointment in marriage, his boredom at work, and his isolation from God. He was light years from where he meant to be at 40 years old. Pat answers and simplistic solutions would not suffice in this conversation—his pain was too deep and too raw. So we found ourselves at that peculiar place of groaning for God to touch yet another situation—and we asked God to, well, find us there. At Denny's. Eating breakfast. In a pool of pain.

Later that day I took a telephone call from another friend whose marriage was in its death throes. His simple, blunt words clearly expressed his pain. The marriage was over. Time to move on. He hoped it was also time to move on beyond the pain.

At the end of the day, I looked again at the business card I had just received. I had hired on to a medical device firm—a company that helped people deal with chronic pain. "Pain Communications, Account Leader," the card read. "Indeed," I thought, "how true. My boss has no idea how this job title fits."

It was a day when the work I was paid for and the work that was my heart's desire intersected. That day a window opened in my friends' souls, revealing the pain of everyday life. And—oddly —a corresponding window opened to reveal the deepest things in my heart. With those friends on that day, problems led to opportunities for conversations about God and how we relate to God. These conversations connected us and made sense to the hearts of my friends, in part because they happened right in the crush of everyday life.

> **Problems led to opportunities for conversations about God and how we relate to God. This is engaging evangelism.**

This is engaging evangelism. And it is the goal of transformation leadership within missional congregations. At the center of it are YOU and me . . . and our willingness to tell the story every day.

Start with Discarding the Unhelpful Snapshots

Evangelism is a multisyllabic church word that has "program" written all over it. And any word that smells of a program gets sent immediately to that part of our brain reserved for the stuff we feel guilty about not doing, along with the boring stuff that's only important to other people. A lot of us don't think of evangelism on our own. More often we need reminding to "do" it.

But if we dropped the word *evangelism* and the baggage it carries—for a time—and looked instead for the windows into our souls that constantly open and shut, we might do better. You see these windows in everyday conversations—like with my two friends. And if we seek a deep, integrated walk with God through Jesus the Christ, the open windows of conversations between friends will pull from our own lives the very things needed, the things God has for us to say, at just the right time. Happily, everyday life is the perfect place for such talk.

Even more interesting, this work of talking about God happens anywhere and everywhere God's people show up. Wherever God's people are—that is, those who seek after God through Jesus Christ—there is a work of God underway. And witness is happening, whether verbal or not. Sometimes it's good witness, sometimes not. But the human condition is such that we always look and watch what is happening in others' lives. We cannot help it. That's why our everyday witness and words work like threads in the daily fabric of many more lives than we'll ever realize. But before we can be free to talk about this work of witness in daily life, let's take a look at the unhelpful images of evangelism that float through our brains—the ones we may even recoil from. If we exorcise these and replace them with more biblical images, we'll be equipped for this lively daily living God has planned for us.

Picture an open-air football stadium completely full. All eyes are cast toward the big-screen TV above the platform. The silver-haired evangelist has worked through the message, given the word that all have sinned, and issued the invitation once, twice, and, in fact, a third time. The band plays quietly. People make their way to the floor. Some want to "do it right" and give themselves to Jesus here. Others have never heard this stuff before. They realize their need to repent of sin, to believe in Jesus, for his words have found a home in their hearts. And so they take the walk. Silence and watching settles over thousands of people as they, too, consider the message.

Now that's evangelism—big time. Everybody knows it. And because it is such big time—often shown on national TV—it's easy to think evangelism is a rare work accomplished by a very rare person. What kind of person stands before thousands of people and asks them to give their lives to this Christ? I'll tell you—an unusual person, someone not like me. The very immensity of the picture would seem to disqualify most of us from ever participating, except maybe within the mechanics of the festival itself: ushering, praying, or counseling, all of which can be good things.

Other images also dissuade us from jumping in—like the plastered-on smiles of white-shirted door-knockers standing before you at your home wondering what you've been thinking about heaven today, or the people compelled to interrupt strangers to talk about God and to keep talking until the stranger takes whatever action they seek. We don't want to be know-it-alls. We would never want to be like them— no, sir. But, in fact, such images are only caricatures of the real work of evangelism.

There's no denying these images inhabit our brains. And although God sometimes uses these ways to help people communicate faith, these images are unhelpful, not because they are necessarily wrong, but because they are not the only ways God uses.

A more helpful image begins with daily, natural interruptions that signal a window snapping open. We don't often see God's hand at work in the interruption because there is no crowd gathered, no stage, no music playing. Plus—didn't this interruption just stop me from my real work? And honestly, we have a stake in not seeing these things. Along with the unhelpful images of crowds and stages and bands playing, the images of people eagerly knocking on our doors make us cringe. We would never want to be as manipulative or as, well, uncool (not to mention unwelcome) as that.

> **We don't often see God's hand at work in the interruption.**

But, in fact, these interruptions and open windows make everyday life a perfect jumping-off point for, let's not say evangelism, but conversations.

So, picture this instead: The woman in the next cubicle, whose urgent and blunt telephone conversations with her husband carry through the fabric walls. Imagine the conversations you have with her once or twice a day about the difficulty in holding a family together these days. "How do you do it?" she might ask.

And you reply, "Man, it is really tough. But my wife and I try to talk to God every night about all the stuff going on. And, in fact, I find myself really drawn close to this Jesus guy—especially when the kids plunged into adolescence six months ago." And so the conversation builds. Was that evangelism? Yes—witness happened. A seed, perhaps, was sown. Productivity depends, of course, on the openness of the ground. But the window snapped open—and two souls communicated about God's works.

Or picture this: Your stylist chats away as she cuts your hair. She talks about how she and her fiancé are struggling with decisions about the house they own. They find they have real differences in how they approach things. You say you did too, early in your marriage. In fact, you nearly split up due to the heat generated by the arguments. You go on, "Really deep issues—for both of us—surfaced around the silliest and smallest chores or undone things around the house. But those were really just an excuse for us to dig at each other."

She says, "Well, you've still got your wedding ring on, so I guess you figured it out."

You say, "Well, we had major help from some folks at our church who— amazingly—had also been through the same thing. Plus," you add, "my husband and I both started being serious about our relationships with Jesus."

"Oh, don't talk to me about religion," she says.

You say, "Listen, I thought the same. But this is different." And on the conversation goes until she keeps cutting and cutting your hair, from short to punk to butch.

Or picture this: Your neighbor, who also happens to attend your church, finds his father quickly declining in health. And then, one Monday morning, his father's gone. Your friend faces the loss of the central pillar in his life. And, for the first time, he realizes his own life is a small, fast race—a race that will someday end. And suddenly he is hungry for more than a liturgy. Or, more precisely, he is hungry for the reality behind the liturgy he says every week. It's easy to see this written on his face, when you talk over the back fence at 8:11 P.M. as you both water your lawns—easy to see because you know your neighbor. And because you went through it yourself, not two years ago, and you talked with this very neighbor about it. It was a tough experience, but now you realize how your faith in Jesus the Christ came alive during that time. And you have great joy in telling your neighbor the rest of your story, and offering to help him see how this story relates to his experience.

The most helpful images of evangelism are those that show one person telling the story of how the God of the universe met them in their pain. Even when the pain still seems unresolved. That's not just more believable—it's also very honest. Those images are helpful, not just because they are easy to tell (no formulas to memorize, no manipulation), but because they are true. Sharing my pain makes me vulnerable even as it connects me with someone. We each have a great wealth of experiences to draw on—experiences of faith that became more grounded in Jesus the Christ because of some need of ours. You might say we groan for God to touch our lives with some bit of heaven, or some bit of healing. And when God does, we should mark the day on a calendar, because we'll refer back to it a lot if we have conversations with other people in this world. God often uses our own deep experiences to tell God's story to others.

God often uses our own deep experiences to tell God's story to others.

Plus, we groan all the time, especially as we age and realize this life is not forever, and as we see the corruption in the world and hunger for peace and joy for our children and for our grandchildren.

Let God Work through Your Groaning

The apostle Paul had a few things he could complain about. His work-a-day vocation was that of laboring over old canvas with needle and thread, making and repairing tents. His avocation found him chased by crowds and stoned, sailing and shipwrecked, bitten by a viper, and imprisoned several times. He had physical disabilities that God didn't release him from until the day he died. He had lofty goals and dreams and visions that spilled out of his relationship with God and across his pages of writing. Paul knew what it meant to groan, longing to be clothed with the heavenly stuff. Probably the more clear his dreams and visions became, the more he longed to be clothed. In 2 Corinthians 5:1-5, Paul wrote:

> For we know that if the earthly tent we live in is destroyed, we have a building from God, a house not made with hands, eternal in the heavens. For in this tent we groan, longing to be clothed with our heavenly dwelling—if indeed, when we have taken it off we will not be found naked. For while we are still in this tent, we groan under our burden, because we wish not to be unclothed but to be further clothed, so that what is mortal may be swallowed up by life. He who has prepared us for this very thing is God, who has given us the Spirit as a guarantee.

We all groan under the burden of mortality. It is the universal human condition. Christians, who have begun to taste a relationship with God through Jesus Christ, and have received the down payment of the Holy Spirit (2 Corinthians 5:5), know more about where to direct that groaning—because of the taste they've had. So Christians groan to be clothed with a heavenly dwelling—especially when life on this planet overwhelms with busyness or sorrows or injustice.

It is everyday life that fine tunes this groaning, what with the sheer hours we can dedicate to worry or work. We each long for the house made by God, that house that will last. Some days we groan for understanding. Some days we groan for our kids. Some days we groan for the people we work with. You could say that everything about our present condition causes us to groan.

There is a larger purpose in the groaning, just as there is a purpose in being in this mortal tent. Our longing is to be swallowed up by life. And this is God's purpose working in us. This longing to be swallowed up by life keeps us longing to be at home with the Lord—for where the Lord is there is life as well. And out of this longing comes the desire to please the Lord right now, even in the groanings. It becomes our ambition, an ambition that takes hold of every day.

Out of Paul's groaning came the desire to be clothed in a heavenly dwelling. Out of his groaning came an ambition to always please the Lord, in every part of his life, because the love of Christ was controlling him (2 Corinthians 5:14) — so much so that he considered his life as given over to this One who paid so much for him (2 Corinthians 5:15). Paul displays his motivation — the closeness of God in all of God's complexity. Paul explains that he takes his groaning into his relationships with others in an attempt to persuade them (2 Corinthians 5:11), because it all adds up to fear of the Lord for him.

> *At the very point God is reconciling us with God, we reach out to invite others to come along.*

Here's the bottom line. Even as we groan our way through everyday life choices and frustrations, God is reconciling us to God's self, as we invite Jesus to make his home in every part of our lives, opening room after room. And at the very point God is reconciling us with God, we reach out to invite others to come along. If they come, reconciliation with God can happen. If they don't come, a seed has been planted and so we become ambassadors from this good country where people are reconciled with God and finally at peace. We taste it ourselves, and that reconciling peace becomes our ticket to discussions with others.

Let God Fill up Your Mondays

But wait, you say. Words like *reconciliation* and *evangelism* belong to the Sunday world. Those words rarely venture out on a Monday. But they can. Let's see how . . .

You rise weary from the weekend — Monday morning, again. You know from Sunday's sermon that your schedule should be open for the living God. But it seems like the pre-dawn hours were made for sleeping.

But the dog is barking so you rise to let him out. And you find yourself using the reason for rising ("God bless our dog," you growl) as time enough to get a cup of coffee and open the Bible. You reread yesterday's Gospel chunk, but already you've begun thinking about the day's meetings, and the work promises needing to be fulfilled. And then you remember the promises made to your son and daughter about helping with schoolwork and soccer practice . . . and that old Monday dread steals over you.

You glance back at the chapter. OK, Jesus is talking about anxieties and how they don't need to be worried over. *Humph.* If Jesus had the life I had, I'd like to see him skip through this day without worrying. You invite him into your day, wondering how he'll handle Monday.

Two hours later you sit in the day's first meeting with your boss and your boss's boss. Your boss has just taken credit for excellent work you dreamed up and delivered. *Humph.* Your mind starts plotting how to get back at him—right there, right in the meeting. But you remember—and this always happens at the most inopportune times—Jesus' counsel was to not resist the evil person, but to turn the other cheek. So just before the meeting ends, in a spirit of let's-see-if-this-really-works obedience, you say to your boss's boss that your boss also is at work on an even more effective program (which you dreamed up without his help or even his knowledge of the problem) and that you were at work on it even this very Monday. Your boss's boss smiles benevolently at your boss, who smiles with raised eyebrows at you.

Monday pitches forward.

Several hours then present themselves for work. You type and think and process, and find yourself really doing something—one of those rare but happy occurrences. As you work, you remember why you enjoy this occupation. The work itself pulls you in. It's interesting—and . . . something else. This feeling of spinning along is not dissimilar to the feeling of . . . well . . . a good worship service. That sounds weird, but isn't God in the details of the work itself, too? Indeed, God is. God's Spirit was on the artisans hired to design and decorate the tabernacle in the Old Testament as they did their craft, and you have something of that same sense. Part of what you are doing right now employs the very gifts you have always thought were given you by God's Spirit, as Paul discusses in his letters.

After lunch (when your colleagues gossiped about your boss and his boss, which you tried to avoid—although a couple of digs slipped out), you hope to get back to that happy state of accomplishing the work you were made to do. You sit at your desk, hands poised over they keyboard, when you hear, "Hey! I need your help with this rush project."

It's your boss, and his urgent project just became yours. And all of your important tasks just slid off the radar screen because this interruption will take the rest of the day. Several more interruptions follow, one after another, and you wonder by the end of the day whether you really did accomplish anything. But two of those interruptions held cries for help. Sandy's marriage is failing, and you found a way to pray with her quietly—but aloud—right there in the cubicle.

You witnessed! But because it was in context, you didn't even realize it until later.

Another interruption found you witnessing to God's direction in your life as you told Jerry, who was passed over for a prime assignment, that when that happened to you last year, you found yourself talking to God—a lot. And later you realized a better thing actually came your way, but you never would have seen it had you not given yourself over to God afresh.

And then, oddly enough, you still don't know where it came from, but you asked Jerry right there whether he wanted to give himself over to God as well. He didn't say yes. But he didn't say no. But neither did he look at you like you were nuts—well, no more nuts than usual. You witnessed! But because it was in context, you didn't even realize it until later.

Just after 5 P.M., your boss comes and sits in your office—right as you are about to leave. The evening's engagements race toward you, but there is your boss, immovable and interrupting yet another part of your life. "Tell me about your faith," he says.

"What!" you think, "Here?" You look at the fabric cubicle walls and add, "Now?" as you sneak a glance at your watch.

"I saw the way you covered for me," your boss says, "and I appreciate it. Being a manager is hard—hard to ever feel like you accomplish anything."

Although you don't have time, there is enough to open a conversation that you know will continue. And in just a few words, before you must race off, the conversation strips you down to the very hope that is lodged in your soul—this hope of Christ raising a dead person, this hope of a touch from God.

Of course, it rarely happens like that. But then again, sometimes it does. And know this: If it doesn't happen in the space of a day, it does in the space of a life, because we all go over and over the examples we've seen.

There is a utility to the interruptions in a day. Oh, sure, they are great momentum-stoppers. But with a quick prayer to the Christ (plus some solid trust in God's Spirit leading the way), it is possible to see interruptions differently. Blessed are those whose personality types love interruptions! But even the rest of us can begin to see the divine hand in what would have been distractions. It is people who are important to God, and God brings them into our lives whether we welcome them or not. It is the very business of life to attend to these people

Summary

I'm considering printing a new business card—one that says more about my real job in this life. Maybe it will read, "Director of Groaning." With a card like that, I'll be free to groan with gusto myself, and I'll be able to direct others to Christ—whether subtly or directly—for relief from their groaning. With a card like that, I'm sure to have plenty of business.

For Reflection and Discussion

1. Has God opened any windows in the last few days for communicating deep things with someone else? What was the conversation about? Did you miss any open windows, thinking they were interruptions?

2. How does your paid or unpaid work fit with the work your soul wants to do? Are they different? Where do they overlap? Is it hard to remember your life of faith at work? Does it seem like faith in Jesus could not be applied to your workplace? Have you ever found yourself filled with joy—like during your best times in church—while you were working?

3. What comes to mind when you think of engaging evangelism? Do those images bring up any emotions? Are those images helpful or not? Would thinking of "conversations about God" rather than "evangelism" be useful?

4. We are always witnessing in some way. When you are not witnessing verbally, how are you witnessing nonverbally? In the last week, were there times when your words and actions reinforced each other? Were there times when your words and actions weren't in line with each other?

5. What do you find yourself "groaning" for? Have you ever found yourself longing to be clothed with "heavenly stuff" and "swallowed up by life" like Paul describes in 2 Corinthians 5? Did you find yourself communicating with others about that groaning? Is it easier to talk with others about areas of struggle in your life or areas of mastery? Which do people respond to more?

CHAPTER 9

Engaging Evangelism in the Congregation

Pat Taylor Ellison and Pat Keifert

Who We Are in Christ . . .

We are lifelong learners. From an early age we did a lot of our early learning in congregations in South Dakota and Minnesota. We continued our learning— Pat Keifert at Valparaiso, Christ Seminary-Seminex, and the University of Chicago and Pat Ellison at the Universities of St. Thomas and Minnesota. These days we learn from one another as we work in, with, under, and against congregations. It has taken time to put what we have learned into practical habits for church people everywhere.

We teach at Luther Seminary in St. Paul, Minnesota, and work with congregations out of Church Innovations Institute. Here, we are called toward innovating our church's capacities to be renewed in mission. This mission and ministry are steeped in listening—listening to God by dwelling in the Word and listening intentionally to those who come to us for help. We believe that only by listening deeply can people be freed to speak with each other and to learn what God has in mind for them. Sometimes we don't hear very well. Sometimes we miss what's really going on. But we never stop listening, and what we hear teaches us about God's mission in the world and within congregations.

Engaging evangelism is in the Christian's job description. Brand-new believers are practically jet-propelled to share the story, proclaiming the goodness of the Lord. Long-time believers and lifelong believers may not take God's love for granted, but we don't think very often of those who don't know God's love for them.

Our congregations are filled with lifelong believers. We are nurtured weekly by our congregation's life and work and consider only rarely the lives of our neighbors who don't join us for Christian worship and fellowship.

But suppose this book is a wild success. Suppose lifelong Christians are inspired to listen to their friends, neighbors, relatives, and coworkers to hear God's story unfolding in their lives and to invite them into lives of new or deeper discipleship. Who will take these newcomers? Our congregations! But what will our congregations do with them?

- Currently, when energized newcomers come into congregational life, eight times out of 10 our first move is to put them on committees. However, only a small percentage of North Americans say that they get energized by committee work.

- Very few congregations have discipleship programs, educational opportunities, or small-group ministries designed for newcomers, although the number is growing.

- Rapidly growing congregations know how to welcome newcomers and invite them into discipleship experiences, but not many have as their goal to create both disciples and evangelists.

- Some congregations have deliberately and serendipitously created space for Christian disciple-making and faith deepening. They also have people in their congregation who can identify spiritual gifts and equip folks for evangelism.

God has a preferred future for every congregation, and the Holy Spirit has already placed the gifts it needs within it. Most of our congregations don't spend much time thinking or praying about the following questions. Yet these are the questions of our future.

- How does a congregation discover its gifts to deepen disciple-ship and equip evangelists?

- What sort of shared vision for mission does such a congrega-tion have?

- How does it tend and nurture that vision in ongoing ways?

- What is the role of pastors and lay leaders in such a congregation?

This chapter addresses these questions through the life and experiences of an imaginary congregation, Ancient and Future Lutheran Church. It is about to receive many newcomers because its people are evangelists who share the story every day and intentionally introduce their friends, relatives, neighbors, and coworkers to the kingdom of God in the person of Jesus Christ. This chapter explores the components of that congregation's capacity to do this intentionally and well.

Plan for the X-Moment

Sheryl is a middle manager at a relatively large corporation. A quiet but friendly person, she is trusted and admired by many. Over the years, she has gotten to know her coworker, Connie. Although they're not best friends, they have shared life's ups and downs with each other. Recently, Connie told Sheryl about a tremendous crisis that has rocked her family. Connie's newly born son, Jason, died from sudden infant death syndrome (SIDS).

Several years earlier, Sheryl, too, lost a child, although the circum-stances of her daughter's death were different. She had never shared this very painful part of her life with anyone at this job.

"We lost a baby girl," Sheryl told Connie one day over coffee. "It was several years ago, but it still hurts." Surprised but deeply moved by this, Connie opened up to Sheryl about her own pain and loss. After a few weeks of short conversations, Connie finally asked Sheryl how she has survived.

"Big parts of my life did not survive," Sheryl said, "including my marriage. But God, a good counselor, and my Compassionate Friends support group helped me survive."

Sheryl's honesty rattled Connie, who grew up in a non-religious home. She avoided the topic for several weeks, but then, one day, she asked, "What difference *has* your faith made in helping you through this horrible experience?"

Conversation that leads to relationship and conversion is a fairly common experience.

"Knowing Jesus made a difference for me," Sheryl said, "because I knew I wasn't alone." Sheryl talked a little bit more about her faith and about how joining a small group of fellow Christians who had also lost children had helped her see that she has the chance for a normal—even full—life again. Connie listened but said nothing more.

A couple of weeks later, over another cup of coffee, Connie asked if she might attend the small group with Sheryl. "Absolutely," Sheryl said, smiling.

After a few weeks of hearing other parents talk about their own pain and loss and the hope Jesus was giving them, Connie asked to explore the Christian faith further. The grief group leader connected her with a seekers' group in the congregation. Over the next few months, Connie decided to prepare for baptism and membership in the congregation. Several months later, Sheryl was a sponsor at Connie's baptism.

Conversation that leads to relationship and conversion is a fairly common experience, according to sociological experts in contemporary conversion. But who really facilitated this conversion? Certainly,

Sheryl's relationship with Connie is important. But if we take another step back, we can begin to see that the main actors in this evangelism story is the congregation. Ancient and Future Lutheran Church has been organized with the purpose of supporting this moment in the lives of Sheryl and Connie—the evangelism X-moment.

X-moments are events for which an organization is organized. At a fast-food restaurant, the X-moment is the two-minute interaction between the server and the customer that is so good that the customer returns. If the restaurant prepares for these moments, they happen often and with excellence.

But often the sense of the X-moment is lost. Often churches see themselves as a family gathered around a pulpit (and sometimes table), with a seminary graduate as the parent or older sibling who is in charge of the X-moment. The pastor is the one who is sent into mission—not the members. The congregation doesn't imagine or organize itself as the *faithful who have been selected, shaped, and sent in the mission of God* into the world of their everyday lives.

Let's imagine that Ancient and Future Lutheran Church is a local church that balances the X-moment of the church gathered with the X-moment of the church dispersed and sent to particular places and relationships with the ability to offer an initial invitation and engagement to those friends, relatives, neighbors, and coworkers who already trust and respect the member of the congregation who has been sent, the apostle.

Our congregation knows its mission and the purpose of the X-moment. We know why we're organized. Our members call folks in, center them in worship of the triune God while learning together, and send them back out into the wide world of work and play. We understand that without Ancient and Future's deliberate attention and support, disciple-apostles like Sheryl would have a much harder time intentionally introducing people such as Connie to the kingdom of God in the person of Jesus.

Of course, Ancient and Future Lutheran Church was not always organized this way.

For many years, we received almost no new members and only a few visitors every year. Several years ago, Karen, a member, launched a small group to help folks handle their acute grief following a difficult death in the congregation. The group was a short-term success, not only for its participants but also for neighbors who were also touched by the death.

Through that experience, our congregation realized we were good at offering hospitality and comfort to the grieving. Before long, several small grief groups developed. The congregation agreed that we had discovered a mission to help people in their grief.

While this discovery was a little bit accidental, we reflected upon it by dwelling in the Word of God and asking if God was calling us to this particular focus in the mission of God. But how could our congregation nurture evangelists like Karen in this ministry? How could we equip ourselves for this mission? These questions led us to reflect on the working pieces of our capacities to intentionally introduce grieving persons to the kingdom of God in Jesus through our existing gifts.

Build Capacity to Do Ministry

To do any job, we need to have a capacity to do it. That capacity has components, just as a book has chapters or a recipe has ingredients. The ingredients of a capacity are:

1. Attitudes and beliefs

2. Knowledge base

3. Skills

4. Habits

If Paul is a woodcarver, he first has to have certain attitudes and beliefs about woodcarving. He has to want to do it and place some value in it.

Second, Paul needs some knowledge about wood and wood products. Next, Paul needs skills for finding, carving, and finishing wood. And he needs habits of work, health, and attention to detail that he can pass on to another person if she wants to learn his craft.

It's the same with evangelism. When we pay attention as a congregation to how we are introducing people to the kingdom of God in the person of Jesus Christ, we realize we would be wise to have certain attitudes and beliefs, minimum knowledge, skills, and pass-on-able habits.

And we must have these things, not just as individuals but as a whole community of faith. The gift Sheryl brought to Connie was given at first through one-on-one, day-to-day conversations at work. But eventually that gift was nourished and Connie was brought into an even deeper relationship with the kingdom of God in the person of Jesus because there was an entire community of believers there to receive her—our congregation.

This chapter looks at the components of capacity desirable for a congregation that is going to receive many newcomers because it has prepared its members for their X-moments—relationships and conversations through which believers introduce their friends, relatives, neighbors, and coworkers to the kingdom of God in the person of Jesus Christ. How does a congregation like Ancient and Future Lutheran Church do that? By developing capacities in these five areas:

1. Deepening discipleship through discerning our call to God's mission both as individuals and as a congregation.

2. Equipping people to introduce others to the kingdom of God in the person of Jesus.

3. Sharing a vision for mission in our congregation.

4. Tending and nurturing that vision for mission.

5. Understanding the roles of pastors and lay leaders in our congregation.

Components of Deepening Discernment

Attitudes and Beliefs

- We care about our relationship with God.
- We desire, even when we're tired, to attend to God's presence.

Minimum Knowledge Base

- We know what disciples do.
- We know what disciples think and feel.

Skills

- We are able to make time for God and God's word.
- We are able to raise questions and wrestle with issues.

Pass-on-able Habits

- We practice daily contact with God in many times and places.
- We practice taking time to dwell in God's word and in prayer.

Deepen a Discernment of God's Call to God's Mission

The first questions Ancient and Future Lutheran Church asked were, "Do we want to deepen our discipleship? What does that look like? What do we look and sound like when we're doing it?" And as we voiced these questions, members became increasingly aware that God was sending them, both individually and as a community, into relationships with others in their community.

It's not enough to have these attitudes and beliefs. What do we know about being a disciple? Our congregation studied the biblical stories about Jesus' disciples—their strengths and their very human failings.

We also got to know more recent disciples, people in our congregation who worship, teach, minister, and trust in the Lord to lead them through the sorrows and joys of life.

Even though it is difficult to make time for God in the midst of our busy lives, learning to do that is an important skill. We learned how to sit at God's feet and listen—or question—or cry.

We learned that we could set aside time with God, but that doing it daily took more than skill. It had to become our habit.

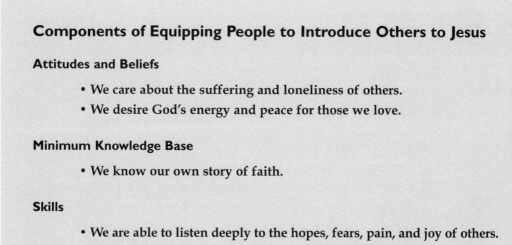

Components of Equipping People to Introduce Others to Jesus

Attitudes and Beliefs

- We care about the suffering and loneliness of others.
- We desire God's energy and peace for those we love.

Minimum Knowledge Base

- We know our own story of faith.

Skills

- We are able to listen deeply to the hopes, fears, pain, and joy of others.
- We are able to hear God's story in their lives and speak about that in helpful words.

Pass-on-able Habits

- We daily listen deeply to one person.
- We daily reserve time to find that person and to talk with God about the experience.

Equip People to Introduce Others to the Kingdom of God in the Person of Jesus

Congregations talk about sending people into the world, but do we really build their capacity to intentionally introduce others to God's kingdom?

At Ancient and Future Lutheran Church, we knew that we cared about people and were good at celebrating joys and honoring sorrows. But that initial group of grief supporters taught us that grievers have long-term suffering. People also began to learn that Karen and this small group believed that God was calling them to minister to and with grieving people and to bring God's peace and energy to them.

Their sense of call spilled out into our congregation. Others became interested in the mission. However, our congregation realized that even though we knew the basics of God's story, we needed other knowledge to connect with people. So, we learned how to listen well and how to talk gently about our own faith stories.

How many of us have not always listened deeply to others before we opened our mouths? How many of us, even when we did learn to listen deeply, didn't speak for fear of intruding or imposing? We have not always had these skills. As a result, we never shared our faith.

After developing these skills, many of us found that we needed to practice, to get in the habit of making time to listen to a person and then talking with God about the experience. Not all have the habit yet, but our whole congregation is working on it together. We talk about it, pray about it, and offer training for the attitudes and beliefs, knowledge base, skills, and habits that support the capacity of equipping people to introduce others to the kingdom of God in Christ Jesus.

Components of Sharing a Vision for Mission

Attitudes and Beliefs

- We believe that God has a job for us.
- We believe that each of us is called to be a disciple.
- We believe that we are called as a congregation to act together for our neighbors.

Minimum Knowledge Base

- We know focus is important.
- We know naming the work gives us focus.
- We know the needs of our friends, neighbors, relatives, and coworkers.

Skills

- We are able to imagine a future in which we do this focused work.
- We are able to name our focus and still listen to others' ideas.
- We are able to discern together God's preferred future for us and follow through.

Pass-on-able Habits

- We regularly compare what we're doing with our vision.
- We regularly pray for God's help to keep our focus and not be distracted.
- We use our vision for mission focus each time we make decisions.
- We regularly pray for the Spirit's help to make clear God's preferred future for us.

Share a Vision for Mission in Our Congregation

Like many congregations, Ancient and Future Lutheran Church has a written vision statement. But it took this experience with Karen and the grief group for a vision no one knew about to become one that members could connect with God's mission in our lives. This shift didn't happen overnight. It took several deaths, several group actions, some mistakes, and quite a bit of soul searching.

As this calling became clearer, our congregation learned that it wasn't set up to support this kind of mission. With 16 standing committees, we found that time, money, and resources were often stretched. But having a clear vision helped us change and focus our resources.

This change was painful, so we developed skills to help ourselves prioritize. Many things still compete for attention. When excellent ideas appear to be outside the congregation's vision, we pray and listen and filter them through the vision. Our leaders share a commitment to being accountable for getting done what they have promised to do.

Over time, these skills turned into habits that became our way of listening to God in our ministry team and council meetings to help us sort through suggestions and make decisions. Sometimes our path is clear, sometimes it's cluttered, but these habits help us get the work done.

Tend and Nurture a Vision for Mission

Our vision for mission is that focus for ministry that we believe God gives us and promises to help us in—not just as individual ministers but through our lives together in worshiping congregations.

At Ancient and Future Lutheran Church, part of that vision is a call to help people in the tough times of their lives, especially when they're dealing with death. Another part is a call to introduce people to God and connect them with a community of believers. An important piece of this vision has been to treat worship as an opportunity for everyone to experience the kingdom of God in the person of Christ.

Components of Tending and Nurturing a Vision for Mission

Attitudes and Beliefs

- We believe that God promises to be present and active in worship.
- We want to focus our congregation's talent and energy.

Minimum Knowledge Base

- We know what newcomers think and feel when they enter our space.
- We know what gives people a welcoming space.
- We know that when people aren't self-conscious, they can be God-conscious.

Skills

- We are able to invite friends, neighbors, relatives, and coworkers to worship and other activities.
- We are able to connect people into worship in a way that they notice God there.
- We are able to connect people to others who dwell in the Word of God and pay attention to what God is doing.

Pass-on-able Habits

- We regularly invite friends, neighbors, relatives, and coworkers to worship and small groups.
- We regularly check with our guests to see that they have a place to sit, something to eat, and someone to talk to.
- We regularly pray for the Spirit's help to serve those we've invited and those we haven't found yet.

But our congregation learned that people who come to worship have different expectations and needs, depending on whether they are regulars or newcomers. Although God promises to be in worship, congregational members realized that we humans can actually prevent someone's introduction to God by distracting them and making them self-conscious.

So we considered what skills we might need to welcome all who come to worship. Hospitality is a skill, and not all members of Ancient and Future Lutheran Church are gifted with it. But some people, often quiet people, have very big gifts for paying attention—for seeing when a hymnal is missing, for smiling at children, for knowing where the bathrooms are, and for being good hosts. These welcoming people are often the best at helping newcomers become more comfortable.

After some time, the congregation realized that these skills needed to become habits in order to be meaningful and effective. Those who have developed these habits really enjoy finding and inviting new people to worship. They find it wonderful to introduce suffering people they know to the ministries at Ancient and Future Lutheran Church. Some of those new people return and some even invite others, connecting them to worship and small groups. The X-moments multiply and God blesses this ministry.

Understand the Roles of Pastors and Lay Leaders in Our Congregation

Ancient and Future Lutheran Church used to have a different idea about the role of pastors and lay leaders. Many saw the pastor as the boss—responsible for all ministry. Others believed the congregation could go as far as the pastor could take it and the laity would allow it.

But our church ran into problems. One pastor burned out. Another was on the verge of burning out. Finally, our congregation realized how to do ministry by and for one another, using our pastors for training, support, and encouragement. But it took an attitude shift, prompted by Karen and her small group, to make us realize that lay people who have

Components of understanding the roles of pastors and lay leaders

Attitudes and Beliefs

- We believe pastors and staff members should equip and encourage lay people.
- We believe laity must lead ministry, with coaching and support from the leaders.

Minimum Knowledge Base

- We know our leaders' gifts and talents and are good stewards of these blessings.
- We know that we are the priesthood of all believers — all believers do the work.

Skills

- We are able to name and clearly describe the work we do and the leader who is necessary to support and organize that work.
- We are able to give our leaders the authority to get things done.
- We are able to hold our leaders accountable for their work.
- We are able to celebrate and thank our leaders for work well done.

Pass-on-able Habits

- We regularly make careful plans, listing resources and time lines.
- We regularly check our plans with our vision.
- We regularly give real authority to make decisions and take action.
- We regularly hold one another accountable for the result, learning from every experience.
- We regularly pray for the Spirit's help to serve those who lead us.

passion and skills for ministry can be great leaders. Although small-group leaders are coached by the pastor, the grief ministry at Ancient and Future Lutheran Church has become an evangelism ministry by laity for laity.

Our congregation found that it helps to know people's gifts and talents. It's better for paid and volunteer leaders, whether clergy or lay, to do the work they do best as often as possible. When labor is needed that they don't do well, others with the gifts to do that work come forward. We know that God calls all of us to work toward God's mission. Martin Luther may have said that we are the priesthood of all believers, but it's quite another thing to know it from experience.

The congregation developed new skills to make this shift. One skill has been to clearly define and focus the work. Then the appropriate leader is almost always easier to find. Sometimes the appropriate leader isn't a member but is a neighbor or friend or a staff member at another church. Another skill has been to be clear about expectations, accountability, and authority. Having authority doesn't mean the leaders do all the work. But it does mean they have the authority to ask for help and expect to receive it. When a task is over, our congregation asks what we learned. Whether it was a smashing success or not, we celebrate, thank, learn, and grow.

By turning skills into habits, our ministry has flourished. We've invented forms that help us do the job, and rituals for accountability and celebration. We even have worship services that celebrate the beginning and end of projects, services that involve song, stories, and prayer.

This looks overwhelming! Does my congregation have to be able to do ALL of these things well? Well, no. Not all of these tasks and skills are necessary for every congregation. Indeed, a key ingredient to engaging evangelism is getting short lists, very short lists, of the minimal attitudes and beliefs, minimum knowledge base, skills, and pass-on-able habits that fit your congregation's call within God's mission.

Summary

Sheryl had just moved to town a couple of years after Karen helped the congregation at Ancient and Future Lutheran Church discover its gifts for inviting persons in deep grief into a caring community. She was looking for a group to help her continue to grieve the death of her daughter and, after her divorce, her sense of family. In a local grocery store she saw a notice for a group that fit the description, sponsored by Ancient and Future Lutheran Church. Even though Sheryl had not considered tying her grief to a church, she felt a deep spiritual need and decided to take a chance on at least one visit to the church's grief group. One visit and she was hooked. With time, Sheryl decided to join the seekers' small group. Eventually, she sought to be baptized and became a member. Some years later, she met Connie . . .

Engaging evangelism meant that someone had to share the story. But it was a congregation—engaging evangelism—that provided the encouragement, training, support, inspiration, and context within which that story could be told.

For Reflection and Discussion

This chapter describes five components of the capacity to invite and receive newcomers:

1. Deepening discipleship through discerning our call to God's mission both as individuals and as a congregation.

2. Equipping people to introduce others to the kingdom of God in the person of Jesus.

3. Sharing a vision for mission in our congregation.

4. Tending and nurturing that vision for mission.

5. Understanding the roles of pastors and lay leaders in our congregation.

For each of the five components of capacity, reflect on the following questions or discuss them as a group:

- What does your congregation believe?

- What does your congregation know?

- What skills does your congregation have?

- What habits does your congregation practice?

CHAPTER 10

Engaging Evangelism in Every Place

Introduction

Kelly A. Fryer

The new pastor was a city kid, called to an open-country church her first year out of seminary. "People are people," she thought, "wherever I go. Right?" Well, yes, of course. But people also live in unique communities, defined by all kinds of things, including geography and the type of community they live in. People in the city, for example, in many ways speak a very different language from people in the country. The new pastor discovered this one Sunday morning when Ralph proudly told her that he had left two gigantic bushels of farm-grown tomatoes on the front porch of the parsonage for her and her family.

"Two bushels?!?" she exclaimed. "Thank you, Ralph. But what in the world am I going to do with two bushels of tomatoes?!?"

Ralph looked at her, puzzled, for a moment. Then he said, "Why, put 'em up, of course."

"Put them up *where?!?*" she asked.

Ralph and this young pastor just looked at each other for a moment, suddenly aware that they were strangers to one another, speaking different languages. A helpful woman, standing nearby and listening to this odd exchange, offered to translate.

"He means that you could cook them up and put them in jars to preserve them. That way you'll have fresh tomatoes all winter long," she said.

The city kid listened, realizing how foolish she seemed to poor Ralph, and broke out into joyful laughter. "What a great sense of humor our God has," she said. "And, wow, do I have a lot to learn!" Her laughter was contagious, and soon the whole Sunday morning crowd was smiling loud about their pastor, who recognized that she was on new ground and seemed so willing to learn from them and about them. She never did "put up" the tomatoes. But her ministry in that place was shaped by the knowledge that, while people *are* people wherever you go, they are also uniquely defined by the type of community in which they live.

Engaging evangelism means understanding the context within which our congregations are located.

Engaging evangelism means understanding the context within which our congregations are located. The things a congregation needs to be thinking about and doing as it participates in God's mission will vary depending on the type of community it serves.

Studies have shown, for example, that for ELCA congregations in rural settings, the single best predictor for whether or not the congregation is growing is *not* population stability, worship style, or having a great Sunday school. It is the ability to develop and sustain a common vision for the future! For congregations in small towns, an increase in worship attendance is directly related to two things: 1) how effective the congregation is at providing ministry with grade-school children, and 2) the extent to which the congregation is held captive by its own past ("But we've always done it that way!").

For congregations in medium-size cities, growth is directly related to how effective the leaders are in planning for the future. The second largest growth factor is that the congregation offers alternative worship. For congregations in large cities, the only significant factor affecting whether or not there is growth is how tightly the membership hangs on to the past. Clearly, there are things congregations need to be thinking about and doing differently, depending on the type of community they are in ("Congregational Diversity, Community Setting, and Church Growth in the Evangelical Lutheran Church in America: Congregational

Characteristics and Practices in Context" by Kenneth W. Inskeep and
Michael Hillary, March 1997. The entire report is available at
www.elca.org/re/reports/context4.pdf).

All that being said, wherever a congregation is located, its "orientation
toward the future" (vision or planning) and the extent it is "willing to
break with the past for the sake of the future are positively and significantly related to changes in worship attendance" ("Congregational
Diversity, Community Setting, and Church Growth," p. 16). This is as
true in the suburbs as it is in the country or the inner city. Congregations
in every place will be engaged in evangelism—and growing—if they are
focused outward toward God's mission in the world (and their neighbors!) rather than inward (toward the needs of their own members and
the preservation of their own past).

Suburban Areas

Craig Bollinger

Pioneering a new congregation has many joys and challenges. One of
the keys we found in growing a church in a suburban area has been to
understand the culture of the people moving into the area and then
translating the gospel message and the experiences of worship and
ministries to address that cultural place.

The abundance of people is not the issue in growing a church in a
suburban area. However, all over the United States churches are growing and closing, including those in suburban areas. In the 10 years I
have been at Christ the King (CTK) numerous churches have thrived
and grown, but a good half-dozen have closed their doors in the same
geographic area. What is going on? Why do some grow and some
decline and close? There are many reasons for decline in congregations,
but in the next few paragraphs I want to share with you some of the
things I believe God is doing at CTK that add to our number daily
(Acts 2:47). We believe God's activity in adding people to this congregation has much to do with creating a climate that people outside of the

church are drawn to, and that people inside the church are passionate to tell their friends about. The climate is one that addresses the natural needs of the human heart that are unfulfilled in the world. As a congregation, we see this type of community lived out in Acts 2:42-47. That early Christian community had a contagious spirit. The people saw the climate and longed to be a part of it. Their growth is best described as "day by day the Lord added to their number those who were being saved" (Acts 2:47).

People will invite their friends and neighbors like crazy when they are crazy about their church.

With that climate as the core, we focus on evangelism. We believe Jesus came to "seek and save the lost" (Luke 19:10). And we know that means *us,* first of all! But we also know that Jesus invited us to be a part of this mission, too (Matthew 28:19-20). We are called to help bring all people to the Savior—Jesus. He, through the work of the Holy Spirit, will change all of our lives and create a heart to follow him. This single passion directs our entire mission and ministries. As we minister through this core purpose and seek to live out our ministry in the spirit of the community of Acts 2:42-47, a climate for passionate evangelical invitation and deep spiritual growth occurs.

Let's think about how the climate is fleshed out in this environment. It is being the kind of church people want to invite people to. I have found that people will invite their friends and neighbors like crazy when they are crazy about their church. In this spirit, people in the congregation know that no matter when they invite their friends or what event or service they invite them to, they can trust that their friends will be received well, have a good experience, and participate in ministries done with excellence. This means that the worship as a whole and the music in particular is dynamic and alive. It connects and bridges the gap culturally with people outside of the church. The messages are relevant, and show biblical application to daily life and our walk with Jesus. The hospitality is genuine and helpful.

Another key to creating a climate and spirit of invitation is making sure people know their friends will be received just as they are. They aren't expected to spiritually be someplace they're not.

At Christ the King, we make sure there is plenty of help, on any given Sunday, for people who are new to the faith and new to church. Classes and small groups are outlined clearly, addressing which are appropriate for people in various places on their faith walk. Spiritual mentors are available to speak with those who have questions before or after worship. There are opportunities to respond if God touches someone's heart in a special way. There are classes offered in which people can seek out answers to their questions. Things like these create a climate where the people of CTK know their friends will have places to get answers and experiences that are meaningful and culturally relevant. When these patterns are consistent, more and more people repeatedly invite friends.

Craig Bollinger has served as the pastor developer at Christ the King Lutheran Church in Charlotte, North Carolina, which organized in spring 1994.

Metropolitan Areas

John R. Sabatelli

"Every Seat Free. Everybody Welcome." So read the original sign at Christ Church in Baltimore, Maryland. Now, 116 years later, the congregation still freely gives away the gospel and welcomes everyone: the rich and the poor; Ph.D.s and high-school dropouts, people of many races, nationalities, and tongues, regardless of sexual orientation. Today, Christ Church ministers to corporate lawyers and highly successful business people as well as to women who are homeless and children who cannot read.

Our evangelism program centers in the knowledge that every human being is a priceless child of God for whom Christ died. Christ Church is called by the Holy Spirit to proclaim the gospel of salvation and to help people live out the gospel of grace in their lives. And so our approach to evangelism does not begin with knocking on doors, which is not an effective strategy in our community, but with excellent worship that is Christ-centered, with solid preaching, great music, and Holy Communion offered every Sunday and Wednesday.

People in this congregation understand and embrace our long-standing commitment to welcome the stranger and to invite those outside the church to worship. This is not the work of the few but of all the baptized. They are grateful to God for what he has done for them in Christ Jesus. They also are proud of their church and want to share all they have at Christ Church in the Lord.

Evangelism and stewardship are part and parcel of everything we do.

The congregation also wants to engage people in ministry, so it gives members and non-members alike many opportunities to share their time, talents, money, and other resources. All are encouraged to serve in our homeless shelter, to volunteer in our local schools, and to work on a task force. New members are so valued that 40 percent of those serving on the congregation council are chosen from among those who have joined the church in the last several years. New blood brings vitality. The seven last words of the dying church, "We have never done it that way," are not part of our vocabulary.

Evangelism and stewardship are part and parcel of everything we do. The staff and lay leadership are committed to reaching out and meeting the needs of the community by being faithful to the gospel and relevant to the material and spiritual needs of the world around us. The job description for each staff member states that daily prayer and Bible study are expected. The staff gathers weekly to share highs and lows and to pray for one another. The congregation's commitment to evangelism can be seen further in its calling of a pastor-evangelist who "lives, breathes, and eats" evangelism. Living two blocks away from the church, he is ever present in the community. He loves the church and people, and he is committed to bringing both together.

God has blessed Christ Church over the decades, and the congregation is always looking for new and varied ways to serve, whether by supporting the rebirth of the Lutheran Church in Russia or feeding children in Bogota, South India, and Papua New Guinea, whether by supporting our seminaries in Gettysburg, Philadelphia, and Tanzania, or by opening a soup kitchen and homeless shelter and starting a nursery school for the children of professionals moving into the increasingly gentrified neighborhood around the church.

"Every Seat Free. Everybody Welcome," says it all.

John R. Sabatelli, a native of New York City, is the sixth pastor of Christ Church in Baltimore, Maryland. He was called to the congregation in December 1982.

Inner-City Areas
Greg Van Dunk

Engaging evangelism in the city begins with immersion in the neighborhood. Many declining city churches are surrounded by neighborhoods teeming with people and their needs. But neighborhood residents will not spend time in the church if we don't spend time in the neighborhood. Evangelism begins with walking around, getting to know people, visiting, and hanging out. Evangelism begins with relationships.

Evangelism in the city continues with church programs that are relevant to the needs of residents. Those programs will most often involve children. They probably will involve food, learning activities, or supervision. For our congregation, a "learn to work" program has been key.

Evangelism in the city requires the firm, loving expectation that participants in our programs (adults and children) will explore and grow in relationship with Jesus through our church. It is common for the church to give away stuff (money, food, clothes, and so on) to individuals with incomes that are low or at poverty levels. Less common for many congregations is the life-transforming dignity and experience of building and being the church with these people. Outreach programs must result in people who are baptized, worship, pray, study, and serve in Christ. We are not doing evangelism if the people we reach do not participate in Word and Sacrament. We are here in the neighborhood to be a church.

Rarely is a pastor in the city afforded the luxury of Sunday schools, vacation Bible school programs, altar guilds, or even ushers, without providing painstaking personal and primary leadership. However, I was recently reminded of what a privilege we have in city ministry. At Sunday worship in our congregation, we prayed for one of our young people and sent him off to a Lutheran college. We had met as I walked the neighborhood. Then his whole family began to participate through one of our programs. Despite huge family troubles, we became the church together and saw incredible transformation and growth in Christ.

Greg Van Dunk has served as pastor and developer of All Peoples Church in Milwaukee, Wisconsin, since 1991. He is the author of Let the Glory of the Lord Rise among Us: Growing a Church in the Heart of the City *(Augsburg Fortress, 2002).*

Multi-Ethnic Settings
George Villa

Becoming multi-ethnic was not easy or natural for St. John Evangelical Lutheran Church in Gardena, California, a congregation located just west of south-central Los Angeles. Changing the infrastructure of the congregation, implementing discipleship guidelines for leaders, formatting worship services to be less Euro-centric, and developing members' spiritual gifts have been key factors in the spiritual and numerical growth of the congregation and the change in demographics to more faithfully represent the surrounding community.

In 1992, the congregation became aware that the community had radically changed. A Hispanic born in Los Angeles, I was called as the pastor to a two-point parish. Both locations had dwindled in size and could no longer call a full-time pastor. The general perception had been that the congregation was still in the suburbs amid middle class, somewhat ethnically diverse people. However, demographic studies showed that the context was definitely urban and ethnically mixed, with no majority group. In my first meeting with the church leaders, I said that the way the congregation "did church" was about to change. Within three months, about one-third of the remaining small membership left.

Several outreach programs were initiated. Teams of callers were trained and sent out to simply invite those who lived within walking distance of the church to drop by for worship. Nearly 10,000 households were reached. Some new families did attend, but more importantly, the callers learned to share their faith stories. Soon, by word-of-mouth within their families, workplaces, and acquaintances, the callers began to invite others to church. Through a mass mailing campaign, high-quality literature reached every household within a four-mile radius. The sanctuary, located on a major street, was painted a brilliant white to stand out to the heavy traffic passing by.

> *The major changes were not a result of the outreach programs but of a change in the culture within the congregation.*

However, the major changes were not a result of the outreach programs but of a change in the culture within the congregation. A written "profile of a disciple" was adopted. Clear expectations for discipleship were used in selecting church council candidates and other leadership teams. The church council formally approved qualifications for church council positions. The *Cursillo* movement was used to help train leaders. A series of seminars was developed on tithing, worship, prayer, and daily devotions, and a whole host of faith-focused training events were held, including lay-led adult Bible studies. Follow-up practices conveyed to visitors that they were truly welcomed and that interest in them was genuine. Some visitors stayed and joined the congregation.

While a traditional *Lutheran Book of Worship* service continued, a second blended worship was started. Developing a praise team and a youth worship team brought different worship styles to the now-growing congregation. A Spanish worship service was also added by merging an existing ELCA Spanish congregation into the overall ministry.

Currently, the congregation's membership is approximately 40 percent Anglo-Caucasian, 30 percent Hispanic (evenly split between the Spanish worship service and the other English worship services), 15 percent Asian, and 15 percent African (a significant number of whom come from Nigeria). Worship attendance has grown to nearly 200 (compared with 58 originally), with a baptized membership of 250. As part of its overall goals for mission, the congregation projects that worship attendance will reach 1,200 in the next several years.

The changes have been multifaceted. In many areas of its life, the congregation had to be dynamically transformed in order to become a living organism and leave behind the dying organization it had become. The congregation's transformation to that of a viable mission outpost has been a miracle in progress, bearing witness to the marvelous things that God is up to.

George Villa serves as pastor of St. John Evangelical Lutheran Church in Gardena, California.

Rural Areas

Nancy Nyland

"Our church building is not in town. Why would people want to come to church way out here?" This question reflected the self-image of a small open-country church. "People will have to drive, will have to go out of their way, to get here." These are the concerns of many rural congregations.

Think about it this way, however. How far will people go to shop, or dine at a fine restaurant, or even eat at a fast-food restaurant? Will they drive 20, 30, or 60 miles? In rural areas they will and they do. So why wouldn't these people drive just as far to go to church? They will and they do. People who feel welcome and incorporated into the church family, inspired by worship, and spiritually fed will drive great distances to be part of that faith community.

My motto has become "If you feed them they will come." We all enjoy a good potluck and the fellowship that surrounds it. But feeding people spiritually is even more important. Gathered as a spiritually fed family of God, a rural congregation can develop into a community unto itself.

As people join together from far and wide, they form a community that is found nowhere else. This community can develop into a place of hope, a safe place to share

Tell people that God is alive in your congregation and that their lives can be different, too.

struggles and grief, a joyous place to share accomplishments, a reviving place to be strengthened for one's daily journey of faith.

Open-country congregations do not have the luxury of focusing ministry on only the surrounding farms and ranches, and small-town congregations do not have the luxury of limiting ministry to the town in which the church building resides. If they do, they will surely miss many opportunities for discipleship. And with a declining rural population, they will eventually die.

So how does a congregation reach out beyond the immediate area or one town? Take out a map and look at the surrounding area up to a 50-mile radius and identify neighboring towns. If you are a pastor, go to these towns, get on the worship schedule in the nursing homes, do devotions on the radio, attend community activities, and shop in the grocery stores. If you are a member of a congregation, put an ad with worship times in the newspapers of these towns, have a booth at town festivals, and attend community activities. Tell people about the great things happening in your church and the great job your pastor is doing. Tell people that God is alive in your congregation and that *their* lives can be different, too. And don't forget to invite, invite, invite. And then, don't be quiet about who you have invited. Ask others in your congregation if they know these people and encourage them to invite the same people. If people are invited by three or four members, they will feel they already know part of the congregation and some of the risk is taken away.

As rural congregations grow spiritually and share the love of Christ beyond the conventional boundaries of their congregations, God will do great and marvelous things.

Nancy Nyland is the pastor at two small-town congregations in Nebraska: St. Peter Lutheran in Bassett, and St. John's Lutheran in Atkinson. She previously served for more than 12 years in South Dakota at First Lutheran, Lake Andes, a small-town congregation, and East Lake Andes Lutheran, rural Armour, an open-country congregation.

For Reflection and Discussion

1. What type of community is your congregation located in? What do you love about living and ministering in this community?

2. What do you agree with in the chapter section on the type of community your congregation is located in? What do you disagree with? What do you have questions about?

3. As you think about sharing Jesus in your community, what works? What doesn't work?

4. What is your congregation doing well in reaching out to people in your community? What do you need to do differently?

Engaging Evangelism with Every People

Introduction

Kelly A. Fryer

L utherans have a long history in this country of sharing the good news of Jesus with various groups of people who share a particular ethnic and cultural heritage. Lutheran churches were built throughout the past centuries by Finns and Danes, Germans and Norwegians—courageous people who left their homes for unknown adventures. Those who settled here, and the generations that came after them, continued to welcome newcomers from these distant shores and helped them make their way in a new land.

But the boats filled with immigrants from northern Europe have long ago stopped arriving. And today, our "funnel vision" (see chapter 5) will lead us to discover that the context within which we are being called to share the good news of Jesus includes a whole bunch of people who look very different from those who planted most of the Lutheran congregations in this country. For that matter, the people in our communities today look very different from those of us who are currently members of most Lutheran churches.

Over the past decade, eight states increased their population by more than one million people. All of these states, which together account for more than 35 percent of the total U.S. population, are in the South and West. These states are Arizona, California, Colorado, Florida, Georgia, North Carolina, Texas, and Washington. And yet, ELCA membership, as a percent of the population, actually decreased in five of these eight fastest growing states over that same period of time. Furthermore, the states in the South and West are among the most diverse in terms of race and ethnicity. In Georgia, Louisiana, Mississippi, and South Carolina, for example, nearly 30 percent of the population is African American. In California, Arizona, New Mexico, and Texas, 25 percent of the population or more is Latino. Lutherans, on the other hand, have been considerably more successful—in terms of sharing the good news of Jesus and building churches—in the distant suburbs of large cities, particularly in states such as Minnesota. In these places, the population is predominantly white and also tends to be better educated and with higher incomes. (This information and related data are available on-line in a study from the ELCA Department for Research and Evaluation: "The Context for Mission and Ministry in the Evangelical Lutheran Church in America," Kenneth W. Inskeep, May 12, 2003. Find the report at www.elca.org/re/reports/re/context5.pdf.)

In recent decades, Lutherans simply have not been able to negotiate the demographic changes occurring in this nation. We are not growing churches in the most diverse parts of our country. And, even in those places where our churches are growing, they are not reflective of the diversity that does exist there. Overall, only 2.5 percent of all ELCA members are African American, Asian, Latino, or Native American, though in places like Minnesota, Iowa, North and South Dakota, and Wisconsin, non-whites make up approximately 12 percent of the population ("The Context for Mission and Ministry in the Evangelical Lutheran Church in America").

If we are really serious about the "special mission" God has for us— sharing Jesus with everyone—it means paying special attention to who "everyone" is. And that means remembering that everyone is "someone." Each individual is a unique child of God who belongs to a community that is a unique creation of God. Engaging evangelism means getting to know these people, honoring their cultures, and learn-ing to speak their languages. It means being open to what they have to offer and the ways in which we will be changed by our relationship with them.

As you use "funnel vision" to look at the context within which God has placed your congregation, what do you see? Who are your neighbors?

It is likely that, among them, you will see people of amazing diversity: African Americans, Arab and Middle Eastern peoples, Asians, Latinos, Native Americans, and recent immigrants from all over the globe. Some of our congregations will see that *most* of their neighbors are people from one or more of these groups. Sharing Jesus with these people will most likely mean radical change in the way these congregations live together and extend hospitality to their neighbors. But all of our congregations, if they are going to be a part of God's special mission, will need to be aware of the issues that are particular to the unique people who live in their communities.

Evangelism among African Americans
Rayford Grady

My faith journey brought me to the Lutheran church because of its theological foundation—authority of Scripture, justification by grace, and the priesthood of all believers. I believe in a reforming church that is central to the sharing of the gospel. The members of Lutheran Church of the Holy Spirit (LCHS) share this conviction, and it propels our mission and ministry.

> **What do we think God is up to in our context?**

LCHS is an African American congregation in the Maple Park, Morgan Park, and Beverly communities on the south side of Chicago. As Christians, as Lutherans, we continually ask, "What do we think God is up to in our context?"

We are the gathered people of God in communities that are predominantly African American and have their own particular nuances, attributes, and concerns. God is reshaping us as a faith community to embody God's mission in a manner that embraces, accepts, and affirms those who are Christians and those who are not yet Christians.

As a faith community within those larger communities, we also ask ourselves, "Where are we, and where are we going?" The answers to these questions help us discern where God is sending us and what we must do to get there. "There" is not a geographical location, but first and foremost a change within our hearts, minds, and spirits that requires openness to the Holy Spirit.

How are we going to be a worshiping community that includes the familiar, sacred sounds and rhythms that also address the concerns that are vital to the communities we serve? These and similar questions — plus challenging proclamations of the gospel and explanations of biblical imagery and narratives — helped LCHS develop a mission statement that reminds, defines, and identifies us: *We are one spiritual body called to make Christ known in our homes, church, community, and in the world.* This mission statement is printed on our bulletins and stationery and recited at every Sunday worship service.

We are now and are becoming a sign of hope that God is concerned for all people.

Our ministries are developed to embody Christ. We are the extended incarnation of Jesus Christ. We are now and are becoming a sign of hope that God is concerned for all people. We are challenged to risk and be risked, to do what is good, right, and just. While developing relationships with others who have mutual community concerns, God wants us to make Christ known by *Caring, Hearing, Relating, Investing, Serving,* and *Trusting.*

God is empowering LCHS with energizing, revitalizing, and convicting passion through God's transforming process. We can accomplish the vision of divine possibilities that the Scriptures mandate and inspire.

The proclamation of the spoken and embodied Word made known over and over again creates many opportunities for evangelism in this context. The doors of LCHS are always open to people in our community. Community agencies use our facility regularly for meetings and training sessions. LCHS is a gathering place for community tutoring, after-school programs, and adult computer training. Our separate 501C3 faith-based corporation has partnerships with several government agencies, and we are presently laying the groundwork for an Early Childhood Development Center.

One example of our church ministry that embodies Word, wonder, and works is "Tuesday's Children." This challenging opportunity is designed around children five to 12 years of age, churched and unchurched, members and nonmembers. Parents bring their children to have fun and play games. All children are invited to use their talents to learn and sing sacred songs, memorize Bible verses, and practice reading prayers in preparation to lead worship every second Sunday. Children invite friends, family, and other children to worship and experience the Word and the works of this ministry. At LCHS, nonmembers and potential members are always welcomed in a context of belonging and love.

Rayford Grady has served as pastor of the Lutheran Church of the Holy Spirit in Chicago, Illinois, for six years.

Evangelism among Arab and Middle Eastern Peoples
Khader N. El-Yateem

I am a Palestinian Christian who came to America to finish my education at the Lutheran Theological Seminary at Philadelphia, then became a mission developer to start Salam Arabic Lutheran Church in Brooklyn, New York, the first official Arabic Lutheran church in America. I was shocked to find that the majority of Christian Arabs had never heard of the Lutheran church in their native country. The people I serve come from Palestine, Jordan, Syria, Lebanon, Iraq, and Egypt. Some are Arab Israelis. The majority of the people come from Catholic and Orthodox backgrounds, rather than Lutheran.

Arab and Middle Eastern Christians have been around since the day of Pentecost 2,000 years ago. Yet, I was surprised when I came to this country and was invited to speak at various events in churches or organizations that the first question I was asked was, "When did you convert from Islam to Christianity?" I always say that not all Arabs are Muslims and not all Muslims are Arabs.

Especially after 9/11, our community has been in the spotlight and under attack, resulting in many people harassed or killed. The first Arab to be killed after 9/11 as a result of hate crimes was a Coptic Christian living in California.

What is God up to in our context? The Arab and Middle Eastern Christians are suffering as a minority both in the Middle East as well as here in America. We trust God and believe that God is with us in the midst of our pain and suffering. Our God is a living God who feels with us and suffers with us. In America we continue to be a minority. We are associated with Muslims and often victimized for that. God in the midst of all this continues to open doors for evangelism. The Arab and Middle Eastern peoples know what it means to be a Christian and what the cost of Christianity is.

> **Our God is a living God who feels with us and suffers with us.**

We continue to turn to God in faith, hope, and trust when a man has been detained and separated from his family because he is from the Middle East. We do the same when a family member is deported and forced to leave this country. We have been doing this for thousands of years and continue to do so for God is with us. We understand God in terms of a liberator, stronghold, defender, rescuer, and suffering servant, and as a God who shows might in the midst of pain and suffering.

Yet God has opened doors of opportunity to reach out and evangelize to the Arab and Middle Eastern peoples. These opportunities could be summarized as follows:

1. Provide language-specific ministries that welcome and minister to Arab and Middle Eastern peoples in their native tongues.

2. Start an English-as-a-second-language (ESL) program.

3. Show an understanding of our struggles and support our causes.

4. Learn about our cultures and traditions.

5. Invite your Arab neighbors to share their personal experiences and struggles.

6. Provide immigration and refugee services.

7. Create resources for the evangelism and outreach of Arab and Middle Eastern peoples in their native language.

Khader N. El-Yateem serves as pastor of Salam Arabic Lutheran Church in Brooklyn, New York.

Evangelism among Asians
George Tan

According to the U.S. Census Bureau, the Asian American population in the United States has continued its growth since the 1980s. This population totaled 10 million at the turn of the new millennium. With its present trajectory of growth, the Asian American population will double to 20 million by the year 2010 and double again by the year 2040 to reach more than 40 million across the United States. If demographic statistics are any indication of our Christian evangelism ministry field, the "Asian American harvest" is certainly plentiful and urgent.

Today the five largest Asian groups living in the United States are the Chinese, East Indian, Filipino, Japanese, and Korean. They all exhibit a similar pattern of adjustment and settlement across the country. Upon arrival, the majority of these Asian Americans initially reside in their own urban ethnic centers, seeking out some form of familiarity and comfort. They then slowly make their way out to the more affluent and secure city suburbs to raise second-generation Asian American children. In general, Asian Americans are gainfully employed in many professional occupations, but their self-determination and work ethics have unfortunately brought on disdain and discrimination by neighboring minorities. The majority of these new immigrants are unchurched, and those who profess the Christian faith are usually uninvolved and untrained for Christian ministry.

In light of the growing Asian American communities in every city across this country, there is a tremendous opportunity and urgent need for Anglo American congregations to reach out to these people for the Lord — not only to witness to our faith in their midst, but to earnestly train them to reach out to their own in Asia. There are Asian American families that frequently return to Asia to visit their extended families. After completing their foreign education, many exchange scholars and international students return to their Asian countries as well. Thus, with Asian Americans we have a two-stage opportunity for our Anglo American congregations to be faithful to the Great Commission: to widen the circle of fellowship in our churches in these diverse communities and to equip our Asian brothers and sisters to bring the gospel to the mission field in Asia.

> *The most basic step in our intentional outreach is to befriend our Asian neighbor, colleague, and classmate.*

With that goal in mind, we have to engage in intentional outreach to the Asian communities in our neighborhoods. How can we be in fellowship with them if we do not have friendship? Therefore, the most basic step in our intentional outreach is to befriend our Asian neighbor, colleague, and classmate. This gesture of Christian embrace can then be strengthened by our generous welcome in meeting specific needs in care and counseling.

Our cross-cultural outreach strategies also demand an understanding of cultural consciousness. We need to learn and accept different customs and behavioral patterns. Then and only then will we have the opportunity to identify, recruit, and train Asian leadership to further advance our local Asian ministries, and fulfill our desire to have Asian missionaries bring the gospel across the seas.

George Tan is the Assistant to the Bishop for Mission Empowerment in the ELCA's Southwest California Synod.

Evangelism among Latinos

Carmen Rodriguez Rivera

When considering evangelism within the Latino community, we cannot deny the impact of the numbers. All demographic indicators emphasize the increasing growth of the Latino community in the United States. Latinos are growing at six times the rate of the rest of the population.

Beyond the numerical facts, we have to discern what God is up to in this context. Although united by a common language, the Latino community is a very diverse group in itself. Our countries of origin are as varied as our skin tones. Our circumstances in this country differ: Some of us came fleeing political oppression, others to improve our economic situations, while some have always been in this country.

As a prophetic community, Latinos bring much to the Lutheran church. The ability to function primarily within family and community is part of our nature. It is effortless for our group to establish a community of faith.

Spirituality is something innate in Latinos, going back to the native religiosity of our pre-Columbian origins. Many of our communal activities revolve around religious events: baptisms, weddings, and funerals. Experiences of racist oppression and poverty have allowed us to develop creative abilities to share our gifts within a community of faith.

Like the widow who offered all she had (Mark 12:41-44), Latinos generously present our gifts—our possessions, our lives, and our abilities—to witness to God's love among ourselves and to the world. In the midst of oppressive situations and suffering, in poverty and displacement, Latino Christians know that, like the widow, it is enough. It is enough to be a participant in the proclamation. It is enough to partake of the sacraments. We recognize that God has accompanied us thus far, and continues to walk with us and guide our way.

In speaking of the pragmatics of evangelism within this group, we must take into consideration language. Although Spanish is more commonly used among the community in general, demographics show us different trends, depending on how long the person has been in this country. Recent immigrants will need to be ministered with mostly in Spanish, and their congregations will be established in a monolingual Spanish context. But, as members of the community establish roots in the United States, a bilingual approach is more effective. The second and third generation is basically fluent in English, while trying to preserve the original language as a means of maintaining their culture and traditions.

We share what little we have with those less fortunate.

Because of our emphasis on community needs as opposed to the needs of one individual, and because many of our members are living within the confines of poverty, Latino communities of faith have always shown ingenious abilities to engage in social ministry. Among other ministries, Latino congregations generally sponsor soup kitchens or pantries, day care centers and nurseries, literacy and health centers, and immigration assistance. Like the widow, we share what little we have with those less fortunate.

This is very important to remember when embarking on the development of Latino congregations. Unlike prevailing wisdom in mainline denominations, we should not always emphasize the monetary aspect or the capacity to sustain buildings and other structures in developing congregations. This is important, of course. In the Latino community, we realize there are financial responsibilities, such as the upkeep of a place for worship, but experience has shown us that lack of financial support, although holding back some of the projects that might be planned, will not impede the proclamation or prevent the administration of the sacraments, and this in itself is what ministry should be.

Carmen Rodriguez Rivera is Director for Latino Ministries in the Commission for Multicultural Ministries in the ELCA.

Evangelism among Native Americans

Gary Benedict

As I was leaving to go to the local nursery for some grass seed, my wife asked me to pick up some mums for her. When I got to the nursery, I knew I was in trouble. There before my eyes were red mums, white mums, yellow mums, and orange mums. They came in big containers, little containers, and medium-sized containers. She told me to pick up mums, but she didn't tell me what kind! Another trip to the nursery was definitely in store.

Abenaki, Apache, Blackfoot, Cherokee, Cree, Hopi, Lakota, Navajo, Nez Perce, Ojibwa, Seminole—these are names of just a few groups of Native Americans, and these groups are all very different from one another. There can be no generic outreach to Native American people as if they were one group. One huge difference is that the Native people of the East Coast have lived among European Americans for more than 400 years in some cases, while many of the Southwestern tribes still have very few European Americans anywhere in sight. One has to always be aware of the context before speaking to any group of peoples. Another thing to consider is the relocation that some of these Native peoples have gone through. Many have been forcibly removed from their traditional home sites into areas that are foreign to them even today. Given all of these differences, how are we to bring the message of the gospel to the Native communities? There are two simple strategies that might help.

First, get to know the people around you. I was talking one night to a Lakota pipe carrier. He is a spiritual person for his tribe. He told me about his home, his people, and their way of life. I told him stories about mine. Then he asked me if I was a Christian, and I said I was. I told him in detail what being a Christian meant to me and how central the Bible was to me. He thanked me for my honesty and then said he wanted to honor me by telling me about his religion. So he told me his sacred stories, and I listened for a long time. At the end of the conversation he said, "I will have to think more about this Jesus" and that is where we left the conversation. It is not our job to save anyone but rather to tell the story of God's love through Jesus, honestly and without apology. It is also our job to honor those with whom we speak and listen to their stories. This is very important to all Native people. Stories are more than fact or fiction for them. Stories are life.

Second, meet on their terms not yours. When Jesus went out to call his disciples, he went into their space. He met Peter while fishing and Matthew at his tax booth. To Native peoples, their ancestral home is sacred and the land itself has importance, so to invite them off of their Holy space to be told about God is utter foolishness to them. Rather than inviting them to church on the first meeting, get to know their land and the places that are sacred to them.

> **This is very important to all Native people. Stories are more than fact or fiction for them. Stories are life.**

When you are invited, walk their holy ground with them and honor their ancestors by being respectful of their ways. After you have honored them by sharing in their space, then invite them into yours. This opens a dialogue among equals rather than a monologue that is hierarchical in nature.

Always remember, evangelism is the brush stroke of an artist.

Gary Benedict is a member of the Odanak band of the Abenaki people. He has lived and worked among several Native cultures in North America and abroad.

Evangelism among Recent Immigrants

Robert "Bob" Fritch

The following is an A-to-Z primer for ministry among recent immigrants and just about everyone else!

Never ASSUME. Our preconceived notions about a culture or a people are generally off target. Never assume that you know how people feel, how things should be done, what people know, or what people will understand. Ask questions instead.

Be aware of BOUNDARIES. While you might become extremely close to another culture, you will never truly become one of them. Recognize and affirm who you are, just as you affirm who others are.

CONTEXTUALIZE. Listen for good ideas and tailor them to the people and to your community.

Learn to DANCE—literally and figuratively. Be able to shift gears and try doing things in a new and different way. Dance to a new rhythm.

Strive for EXCELLENCE in everything that you do, prepare, send out, and say.

To FAIL is human. Not everything will work, and that's OK. Grow from it and keep trying new and different ways.

Live by GRACE. People might ask you to do things that are different, ritually and liturgically, from what you grew up with. That does not make those things un-Lutheran or even un-Christian. Temper your decisions with a dash of grace.

Go to their HOMES. In the home countries of many immigrants, the pastor could visit most of the parish in one day by simply walking up and down the road. Visiting is not only expected, it is demanded. Go and go often.

Throw away the word *I*. It is not about you — it is about them.

Do not be JUDGMENTAL. Simply because something or someone is different does not make them wrong or problematic.

KEEP trying. A mission-oriented church cannot help but grow.

LEARN all you can about what their lives were like back home — their families, likes, dislikes, fears, and dreams. Learn the geography and the politics from their perspective. If English is not the primary language, learn as much as you can.

What would MARTIN do? Consider that those joining you for worship might not have ever heard of a Lutheran before. They might not be Christian, and they might not have ever set foot in a church before. How do you welcome them into worship?

NAME them. Learn their full names, the name that people call them, how to spell their names, and most of all, how to correctly pronounce them.

OBSERVE how people interact with each other. Observe the social customs and rituals, how people greet each other, and how they say good-bye. It is a mark of respect to greet them as they would greet each other and be respectful of the things the people do not do as well. (For example, in some cultures it is inappropriate to hug, especially for a man to hug a woman.)

Church is not about PROGRAMS. Programs might get them in the door, but if you are not truly the church for them, they will leave.

Emphasize QUALITY in everything you do.

Throw away some of the RULES, especially for weddings, funerals, and baptisms. What would happen if the church stopped saying no to people and said yes more often?

Be SENSITIVE to the people's needs, both culturally and liturgically.

TRANSITIONS are important. Be present not only for weddings and funerals, but also at births and the day of death, new homes and new cars, and birthdays and anniversaries.

UTILIZE the leaders God has provided. Train them, encourage them, and pray with them.

Celebrate every VICTORY. Let people know the good things that are happening. Let them know over and over—it will become contagious.

WORSHIP is the most important ministry you have—the portal to your church for newcomers. Good, solid, well-led worship is key to an inviting ministry.

EXPLAIN things to people. If worship is the portal, do you assist newcomers through it? Tell people how things happen, who is invited, where to go, what to sing, and what those little numbers on the hymn board mean.

YOU are not alone. Ask for help from colleagues who are in similar situations. Read, go to conferences, visit other churches, and learn all you can.

Be ZEALOUS for the gospel. There is a hungry world out there dying to hear the words of eternal life. Feed them!

Robert "Bob" Fritch is pastor of Our Saviour Lutheran Church in Jamaica, New York.

For Reflection and Discussion

1. Think about the people who founded your congregation. Who were they? Where did they come from? Were they intentional about sharing Jesus with people from a particular cultural or ethnic background? Why did they do this? What were the results?

2. What cultural or ethnic groups live in your neighborhood today? How is your congregation doing at sharing Jesus with them? (In other words, does the cultural and ethnic make-up of your congregation really reflect the community within which you live?) If you're not doing very well at this, what is stopping you?

3. God has placed you and your congregation in a particular context because you have something the people there need. But God also wants to use them to change you! How would you and your congregation be different if you really welcomed and invited *all* your neighbors? How would people of diverse cultures and ethnic backgrounds change you? Is this scary for you? Or exciting? Why?

4. Who can help you understand more deeply what it will mean for your congregation to really share Jesus with *everyone* in your community? Invite them to spend time with you and the leadership of your congregation. And pray for courage to do whatever Jesus is calling you to do!

CHAPTER 12

Engaging Evangelism in a New Day

Andy Hagen

Who I Am in Christ . . .

I am a pastor. I have been called to care for the sheep in my fold. But the Good Shepherd has also called me to lead a congregation that cares for the lost sheep at Joyful Spirit Lutheran Church in Bolingbrook, Illinois.

I am a missionary. My mission field has been my own backyard, the post-Christendom, postmodern culture that I live in.

I am a lost sheep. Being lost is what I have in common with the rest of the sheep. I just happen to know that the Good Shepherd is dying to find us.

I feel like a total geek when I say this, but my confirmation day was one of the greatest days of my life. My experiences in the church had prepared me well to make the commitment to follow Jesus. I had been blessed by faithful parents, inspiring mentors, encouraging teachers, and wonderful opportunities to grow in my faith through ministry and learning. When I said, "I do, and I ask God to help and guide me," those weren't just words, they meant something to me.

But when I showed up for worship the next Sunday, I was surprised. As I looked around, I could not find a single one of my confirmation classmates. And for the next four years until I left for college, I would rarely or never see them again. I missed them and was saddened by their exodus. Apparently what was a new beginning for me was some kind of ending for them.

What if those who left haven't or won't come back?

With a wink and a nod, our parents and our churches probably said, "They'll be back. In a few years when they've settled into a job, come back from college, or gotten married, they'll be back." Congregations were confident that when kids finally settled down they would come back to church. Parents were convinced that one day their children would bring their grandchildren to the font and that the cycle would continue.

But what if the cycle is broken? What if those who left haven't or won't come back? In a report titled "The Context for Mission and Ministry in the Evangelical Lutheran Church in America" (Kenneth W. Inskeep, May 12, 2003) the ELCA Department for Research and Evaluation points out this issue:

> In the late 1960s and early 1970s, large numbers of young people who were baptized in the church began to defect. This large scale defection has had serious implications for all mainline denominations. This generation, particularly those born in the later years of the baby boom, is much more likely to think of participating in organized religions as optional, something to be purchased (or not purchased) as it is needed, or when it is appealing.

We confidently assumed that baby boomers (born 1940-1964) would return after they got Woodstock, Vietnam, and other toxins out of their systems. Many did not. And many of those who did come back did not find what they were looking for. The world had changed, and their congregations had not kept pace. Boomers had tasted of alternative spiritualities, moralities, and lifestyles. They went back to church to find business as usual and a lime-green gelatin salad with carrot shavings in it. So they had their babies and did not continue the cycle of returning to church. Many of their children, the so-called Generation X born in the mid-1960s and 1970s, have had little or no exposure to the church. And now they are having children, another generation raised outside the church. This chapter will explore what has happened to our relationship with those generations that are not returning to Lutheran congregations and what can we do about it.

Be Willing to Bridge the Distance

My aunt belonged to a church that required women to keep their heads covered at all times, yet she would never think of wearing a hat to work or when she was out shopping. So on Sunday mornings, she popped the trunk, got the hat out of its box, put it on, and walked into worship. She belonged to two different cultures with two different sets of values and goals. To outsiders this might seem kind of weird but she was used to it.

While this seems humorous, don't we all put on different "hats" for church than the ones we wear at work or home? Are we aware that when we go to church we act, talk, see, and even think differently? For example, in our churches we expect people to sing without a beer in their hands, juggle three different books and a bulletin while standing up and sitting down at strange intervals, give money without getting something for it, read an old book that is full of contradictions we can't explain, and do all of this in a room covered in angry red carpet sitting on uncomfortable chairs without cup holders! And don't forget the lime-green gelatin with carrot shavings in it. For many of us, commuting between two different cultures on Sunday morning is natural. Even if we notice that it is kind of weird, we are used to it.

Those who do not commute between cultures but live solely in the post-Christendom, postmodern one, think this is all very weird and can't imagine getting used to it. They don't have a hat, they don't want to put one on, and they can't imagine why they would ever want to. Some used to have a hat, but it doesn't fit well or is no longer stylish to them or to the world. Others have never worn a hat. (For men it is just the opposite. Men who come to my church never think to take off their baseball hats in church. Why would they? That would be weird!) We cannot reach people in the post-Christendom, postmodern culture if we don't understand how weird the church context seems to them.

This is perhaps the biggest obstacle we face in reaching those who have left our churches. We need more than the desire to reach them. We need a willingness to bridge the distance between the culture within and the culture outside. Curiously, we don't seem to mind the effort to bridge this distance for those in other countries. I have attended global-mission events where Lutherans enthusiastically clap and even sway when songs from foreign lands are sung. I have also attended conferences featuring "contemporary music" where Lutherans had to be probed for signs of life. Global mission is safe. Local mission is dangerous. We might have to find room for a drum set by the altar! Or we might be asked to lead a small-group Bible study!

Understand and Love "Post-er Children"

Although we all experience the influence of the emerging post-Christendom, postmodern culture, those who were born after the mid-1960s have completely grown up in it. They are the "post-er children" for this new culture. What does this culture look like and how has it influenced the way people see the church and faith?

Post-Christendom

Since the Roman emperor Constantine's official acceptance of Christianity in A.D. 313, the relationship between Christianity and the surrounding cultures has been significant. (It's interesting to note that my son can study Christianity at school only because of its undeniable influence on Western history.) The church molded and shaped the culture with a powerful influence on politics, morality, commerce, and daily life. Our parents and grandparents in this country would not have hesitated to consider this a "Christian nation."

Today there are signs that this historic influence of Christianity upon culture is waning or at least changing.

- Stores do great business on religious holidays.

- My children have never had a Christmas program at their public school.

- The car wash in my town often has a line down the street on Sunday mornings.

- Our youth members think Martin Luther was a 1960s civil rights leader.

- My daughter's soccer games started before noon on Sundays last year.

- The best-known Christmas carol at our church would be "Rudolph the Red-Nosed Reindeer."

- When our members tell their friends that they go to church most ask, "Why?"

- In the congregation I serve, some new members don't know who Saul, Isaiah, Ruth, Ezekiel, or Leah were, and they think Ahab was a whaler, Paul was a Beatle, and Judas was a priest.

- At Christmas, our community displays a crèche, a large Hannukah candle, and a "Happy Kwanza" sign on the front lawn.

- Clergy members are not automatically considered community leaders, as they once were.

- Churches struggle for zoning permission.

- Most people feel the church should stay out of politics and morality.

For our parents and their parents, membership in the church had cultural supports. In a Christian culture, those who drifted away from active church life as young adults found themselves nudged back in many ways. Brides envisioned weddings in church sanctuaries and new parents felt internal and external pressure to bring the baby to the font as soon as possible. There wasn't much to do on Sunday mornings except go to worship. Social relationships and events were tied to the church. Positive images of the church were the norm in the media. The church was seen basically as a "good" thing and not belonging to it was a "bad" thing.

We can no longer count on the cultural supports that used to be in place to encourage church involvement. There are more things to do on Sunday morning than worship, a personal crisis no longer prompts a call to the pastor, church membership is no longer a sign of respectability, and the Bible is only one of many inspirational texts available. When we say that our current culture is a post-Christendom one, we say that the church's influence is no more and perhaps even less than other organizations and ideologies in shaping our culture.

In a post-Christendom culture, those who leave the church are not nudged back and may even be commended for escaping. Brides envision weddings in bird sanctuaries, and new parents feel pressure to get their newborn into swim classes. Sunday mornings are filled with sports and brunch and lawn mowing. Social relationships and events abound outside the church. Negative images of the church have become the norm in the media. Belonging to a church may be seen as a good thing, but not belonging to a church is not a bad thing—and could even be a good thing, too.

From Modernism to Postmodernism

Many experts agree that we are also living in a *postmodern* culture—that long-held *modern* beliefs are coming to an end. The *modern* worldview, which surfaced in the 1500s, offered to carry the world toward a glorious new future created by human reason and initiative. Long gone were the Dark Ages, and religious superstitions that had held back the human spirit! Scientific exploration brought knowledge, knowledge brought power, and with that power we could change the world for the better. Confidence in the modern view grew as the world was mapped, diseases were treated, and individual liberties were gained.

Although this was a humanistic view of the world, modernism influenced Christian thinking in many ways. God, the Creator, stepped back from daily life only to "help those who help themselves." Revelation was replaced by reason, faith by dogma, community by individualism, religious experience by theology, and discipleship by membership. For Lutherans, the Reformation and its aftermath are fully entwined with the modern worldview. The same printing press that gave birth to the modern age brought the Bible into people's hands to interpret God's Word for themselves. The rejection of papal authority ushered in the modern understanding that authority resides in the convictions of each individual. The Christian church, though fragmented, optimistically pursued the Christianization of the world.

> *Postmoderns are seeking ways to live within the reality of a broken and confusing world.*

The *postmodern* worldview brings into question the foundations of modernism. The unreserved optimism of modernism has been checked by caution. The modern world failed to feed the world or end warfare, gave birth to the Holocaust, poisoned the environment, and produced alienated and depressed people. Postmoderns, therefore, reject the core belief that human reason and effort will create a utopia. Instead, they are seeking ways to live within the reality of a broken and confusing world.

Postmoderns value experience over reason, diversity over conformity, community over individualism, acceptance over tolerance, and compassion over idealism. Postmoderns are suspicious of the modern claim that there is such a thing as objectivity, truth or that one overarching philosophical narrative can and will be discovered. Rather, postmoderns embrace subjectivity, relativism, and pluralism. How the postmodern worldview affects the worldview of those in our times varies and no one can be certain how long it will be influential. But it is clear that our churches are already experiencing the challenges this worldview brings:

- Postmoderns have a growing interest in spirituality, but they are not sure the church has anything to offer them.

- Postmoderns are interested in finding places where they belong, but they are very suspicious of institutions.

- Postmoderns desire deep and meaningful relationships, but they find that most congregations do not foster such relationships.

- Postmoderns are interested in developing faith, but they have an aversion to dogma, especially when it does not allow room for insights from other sources and experiences they have had.

- Postmoderns are interested in the Bible but they will not accept that certain things are irrefutable just because they are in the Bible.

- Postmoderns might go to worship to have a spiritual experience but not out of duty or habit.

- Postmoderns are not interested in serving to maintain an organization but rather to make an impact on the world.

Challenges and Opportunities

The "post-er" culture offers serious challenges and exciting opportunities to congregations. Our congregations have depended on a Christian culture to bring back their children, but we shouldn't expect those in the post-er culture or subsequent generations to return to church out of a deep-seated conviction or even shallow habit. They are not bad people. They are not lazy people. And they are not heathens, yet. But they live and breathe in a post-Christendom, postmodern culture that no longer sees involvement with a church as a given.

At the same time, many who have sought to reach out to these post-er generations are convinced that this will be a great time of blessing for the church. When Christianity is no longer confused with the broader culture, the gospel may speak more clearly than ever. Being a Christian in a post-Christendom time may be challenging, but it may more closely resemble the experience of the early church, which developed passionate, committed followers of Christ.

As we try to reach the post-er group, we may be surprised to find that they speak a different language. While it may sound like English, it is every bit as strange to our ears as any foreign language. It is a language developed within a post-Christendom, postmodern culture. There are many reasons to hope that we can enter into a dialogue with those who have left the church—if we are willing to learn the language they understand. And there is every reason to believe that God wants us to do this and will bless our efforts.

Most of our churches do not have cultures that are postmodern friendly. Members who experience good news and grace in their congregations are often startled to find out that they appear strange and irrelevant to the post-er children outside. In return, we may find ourselves criticizing them, resenting them, or giving up on them. But we cannot. They are our children and God's children.

God is brewing up something potent in these times. In the challenges present in our post-Christendom, postmodern culture, we may find many exciting opportunities for renewal and new life. What does God have in mind? It may not be a bigger ELCA. It may not be saving our congregation from extinction. But it just may be the redemption of the whole world that the Creator has made!

Resist Doing Business as Usual

Reaching out in the post-Christendom, postmodern context has been a wonderful and frightening adventure for me. When I began developing Joyful Spirit Church in Bolingbrook, Illinois, in 1993, I was only dimly aware of the implications of this context. I grew up in a strong Lutheran culture and was trained to serve it.

Yet I intuitively knew that "business as usual" in our churches was not cutting it among many of those who were my age and younger. Worship needed to be more experiential, relevant, and energizing. Fellowship needed to go beyond coffee hour to building community. Serving meant using your hands, not simply writing a check. Faith development was not just for children but for all ages and for their whole lives. I made the decision to focus our ministry on reaching my former confirmation class-mates who had never come back to church.

It was a joy to watch our congregation grow primarily by bringing back those who had left the church. When they began to connect with our ministry, they would tell me that they never knew church could be fun. They liked the welcoming atmosphere we worked hard to provide. They felt comfortable in a worship experience that was upbeat and relevant to their lives. They were growing in faith, hope, and love through our small groups and ministry teams. Joyful Spirit was not

We are longing to have young people in our church again! How can we get them to come?

Well, first, consider your motivation for reaching out to post-er children:

- Do not reach out with a goal of filling the growing void of youth and young adults in your congregations. Do not desire their partici-pation to gain members or volunteers or giving units. They are completely uninterested in your numbers and will resent being considered one.

- Do not seek them to save them from an eternity in hell. That's the work of the Holy Spirit. Seek them because you want to share the blessings of faith, as you have known it in your life.

- Do not seek the lost because it is cool. This tempting fad treats them as means to an end. They deserve more than that.

- Do not seek the lost out of guilt or fear. If God wants the church to prevail, God will take care of it. In Jesus, God already has! But what a joy it is to work with God.

an overnight success. It took nine years of worshiping at a school before we were able to build our modest ministry center. But we are grateful to have been given the opportunity to start fresh with a focus on the post-er children.

I made many mistakes. It is not easy to grow up in one culture and try to serve another. It is a lot like being a missionary in a foreign land. I thought if I jazzed up "A Mighty Fortress," post-er generations would sing it with the same gusto my home congregation did. I was surprised to find that attending worship once or twice a month was considered to be regular attendance. I thought that once they "got it" they would stop swearing and telling dirty jokes. I believed that once they were no longer intimidated by the Bible they would read it more. I was confused to find that people who were actively involved in our ministry for years did not want to become members. I underestimated how hard it would be for them to feel comfortable enough to invite their friends. Yet each of these realizations taught our ministry more about the post-ers we were aiming for and how we needed to shape our ministry to serve them.

Starting new congregations is one way for our church to reach post-er children. Mission developers who are post-er children have a better understanding of and passion for reaching their friends, and it may be easier for newer congregations to develop a culture that is open to post-er children than for existing congregations to transform their cultures. We should not think that this is easy work, however. Starting new congregations in this context will be increasingly difficult and will require greater support and resources than ever before.

Our greatest potential lies in reaching post-ers through our current congregations. For some congregations it is too late, for others it will be too hard. But for many a change of heart, an opening of eyes, and a reaching out of hands will reach those who have left. The remainder of this chapter sketches a practical approach for creating a church culture that is more in tune with the larger culture we now live in.

I. Develop relationships with post-ers

Any effort to reach those in their 20s and 30s should begin by building relationships with them. In this age group, those who are very active and involved in your church have learned how to put the "church hat" on, but they take it off at home, work, and play. Gather them together, talk about their missing cohort, and ask for their impressions, opinions, and ideas. At the same time, look for those who come rarely or stand at a distance. They have been less successful or interested in accommodating and may have even sharper insights. When some level of trust has been developed, ask them to invite their unchurched friends to a local coffee shop, restaurant, or bar for an open conversation about the Christian faith and the church. The advantage of this approach is that it starts with people instead of programs.

2. Connect with post-er culture

Examples of post-er culture are not hard to find; just turn on your TV or drive to your local video, book, or music store. Ironic and irreverent, spiritual and satirical, dark and humorous, post-er culture can be hard to appreciate for many of us. But we must make some effort to watch, listen, and learn. If we do, we will find that there are many, many points of contact between the Christian faith and post-er culture. Our best guides to this culture may be our own youth groups or college students. Invite them to suggest a movie and then watch it with them.

Many of us are too busy or uncomfortable to hang out at coffee shops or the mall. Yet it is at these gathering places that we can discover what post-ers are doing and saying. The same can be said of local bars and music clubs that attract post-ers. Perhaps a local college chaplain would be willing and able to connect you with some students who could show you the ropes. Go as a loving observer, one who is passionately interested in making connections.

3. Check out resources on post-er ministry

A quick search on Amazon.com for the key word *postmodern* finds more than 1,100 books on the subject. It's time to get busy! Check out books on ministry to post-ers, such as the following:

- Brian McLaren, *A New Kind of Christian: A Tale of Two Friends on a Spiritual Journey* (San Francisco: Jossey-Bass, 2001) and *The Church on the Other Side: Doing Ministry in the Postmodern Matrix* (Grand Rapids, Michigan: Zondervan, 2003).

- Tony Jones, *Postmodern Youth Ministry* (Zondervan, 2001).

- Chuck Smith Jr., *The End of the World . . . As We Know It: Clear Direction for Bold and Innovative Ministry in a Postmodern World* (Colorado Springs, Colorado: WaterBrook Press, 2001).

- Gene Edward Vieth Jr., *Postmodern Times: A Christian Guide to Contemporary Thought and Culture* (Wheaton, Illinois: Crossway Books, 1994).

Choose from numerous annual conferences that focus on post-er culture and ministry. Also, you will find very few conferences that do not offer these topics in their breakout times. Among the many magazines marketed toward this culture, *Relevant* by Relevant Media Group makes the effort to address "God. Life. Progressive Culture." Probably the best way to see what is out there is to do what post-ers do—surf the Internet. Also visit www.emergingchurch.org, offered by Karen Ward and Nathan Frambach, two Lutheran leaders at the forefront of postmodern ministry. This site offers many links to other quality sites and to churches that share their passion.

4. Seek out those involved in post-er ministry

Nothing has been more helpful to me than visiting those churches that are intentionally targeting their outreach to post-ers. I have found leaders and members of these churches to be excited about sharing their vision and experiences with others. In addition to attending a worship service, try to meet with the staff members and sit in on a small-group meeting. The Emerging Church Web site offers a listing of congregations throughout the country that you may consider contacting. Consider recruiting a team from your church to go get a firsthand experience of what post-er ministry looks like. No church should seek to copy another's approach as we all have our own context and character, but we can learn so much from those who are out there on the edge already.

5. Prayerfully consider ministry changes

If you were expecting a laundry list of programmatic changes to make, you are by now thoroughly disappointed. Congregational culture must change in order for techniques to be effective. It would be silly to think that offering *lattés* at the coffee hour will bring in hordes of post-ers if the congregation doesn't want them to come. We do not want to make the mistake of changing what is on the surface but not what is deep down. Post-ers know the difference. With that said, there are certain ministry changes that can assist with such a culture change.

- *Worship life:* Do people feel engaged, are all their senses stimulated, is there an expectation that God is present and something is going to happen in worship? Congregations where people *worship* instead of simply *attend* a worship service are more likely to interest post-ers.

- *Preaching:* How does this seek to connect with the current culture? Are there illustrations and references intentionally aimed toward younger adults? Is the preaching dogmatic or does it seek to inspire the congregation to go on a journey of faith?

- *Community:* Will post-ers find this at our churches? Are groups open to new participants? Can new groups develop? Social events that post-ers can bring their friends to may challenge our traditions—and perhaps they should.

- *Service:* Post-ers aren't interested in maintaining the institutional life of our congregations but they are interested in serving. Post-ers at Joyful Spirit who ignored or resisted our regular pleas for more "greeters" or "nursery aides" have shown great excitement for our mission trips to Haiti and hands-on community projects.

- *Leadership:* Seek, encourage, and develop post-er leaders in every area of your ministry. Then protect these people from the resistance that is sure to come from other leaders as they begin making changes to reach their friends.

Summary

As I look at Joyful Spirit, I wonder if it is the kind of place that could welcome back my former confirmation classmates. The answer is clear — maybe. The congregation is full of post-ers and their children. They have come back and some are even bringing their friends with them. But we are only reaching a small fraction of the post-ers in our community. Some drive by our church without even the vaguest thought that this or any church could make a difference in their lives. We have a lot of challenging work to do. So do many Lutheran congregations across the country. And I am confident that God will bless our efforts to reach post-er children.

For Reflection and Discussion

1. Can you relate to this description of the "new day" we are in? Are you one of those who did come back? Are you one of those who hoped your children would come back? Are you discouraged or challenged by this situation?

2. What are your motivations for reaching those generations that have left your congregation? What can be done to your church culture to develop motivations in tune with what God desires?

3. To see just how weird our church culture may appear to others, ask some 20-somethings who don't go to church to visit your worship and church events. Then ask them to share their honest impressions of what they see and experience in comparison to their own culture.

4. In a post-Christendom culture, there are fewer cultural supports for church commitment and involvement. Have you seen this in your own life? How do you think this affects the generations we are losing from the church?

5. How willing is your congregation to try to understand this post-er culture? How willing are you? What attempts have you and your congregation made to do so? How willing are you to change things in order to help these new generations hear the story you have to tell? How willing are you to listen to *their* story?

CONCLUSION

Where to Next?

Jon V. Anderson

Who I Am in Christ . . .

I have been blessed by many different angels proclaiming the good news
to me through their actions and words. When I went to college, I got lost in
my faith life and in other ways. A friend named Jeff helped me reconnect with
a Christian faith community at a crucial moment in my life. He listened to my
spiritual struggles and invited me to a smaller, less formal worship experience
at college. There I heard authentic preaching that broke through my walls.
I enjoyed a deeper sense of community and experienced grace in a variety
of ways.

God tipped my life in those moments of conversation, worship, and individual
reflection. God continues the process of evangelizing me, day after day, week
after week, month after month, year after year. Even today God continues to
turn me around, lift me up, open my eyes, and inspire me to love as I have
been loved. I give thanks that God's Spirit is patient, stubborn, and relentless
in working to shape us into the ones we were made to be.

As I write this chapter, I am in the opening days of serving in the office of
bishop in the Southwestern Minnesota Synod. I have a lot to learn. We all do.

God's up to something new. All across the country, people are pausing to pray at noon. We sit in offices, on tractors, in chapels, sanctuaries, and cars. We pray that God might deepen our commitment to be *evangelical witnesses*. We are praying for our church. We see faces of friends, family members, and neighbors in our minds as we pray. We ask God to send someone to communicate the good news to them . . . and to us.

Have you noticed? Lutherans are beginning to talk about evangelical witness. We are trying to understand why engaging evangelism is so hard for us. We are facing our sin of not being bold in telling the story and sharing the good news that God has given us. We hear God calling us to turn around. We are looking for opportunities to speak about our faith in words and through body language. God plants in us this longing to go deeper. God's Spirit opens our ears to the gift and the call to follow Jesus. We are recognizing that part of being an apprentice of Jesus includes witnessing to the good news. God is up to something.

It Is Time to Refocus

What you focus on really matters. My wife, the artist, has taught me that in her painting and photography. If we continue to focus inward, we will continue to wrestle ourselves deeper into darkness and despair. If our congregations focus on taking care of our members, we will never have time and energy for the broader ministry and mission we were called to by the Lord of the church, Jesus Christ. We can choose to focus

Evangelical Witness

Marcus Kunz, a Southwestern Minnesota Synod Minister, argues that the term *evangelical witness* is more helpful than the word *evangelism*. When we are witnesses, we proclaim the truth as we know it. Then we trust God to do the work.

on the past, but we risk failing to see where God's Spirit is calling us *now*.

Just imagine what might happen if we focus together on the question, "What does it mean to be faithful and fruitful followers of Jesus *now*?" The stakes for people are so high that God's Son came into our midst, suffered, and died on a cross to reach us. A God who can twist the death of Jesus on a cross into a sign of forgiveness, resurrection, and hope can transform people who will change churches and care for and love God's world. Our crucified and resurrected Lord calls us to focus on our mission and ministry as baptized ones, congregations, synods, and the ELCA.

It Is Time for Change

Question: Do you know how many Lutherans it takes to change a lightbulb?

Answer: How dare you change that light bulb when my grandmother gave it to the church 27 years ago.

People laugh at this joke because they recognize the danger of treasuring the past so much that we fail to keep our eyes on the light that is leading us through the darkness. They laugh because they remember conversations that were that absurd. They can laugh instead of crying because they know that "memory is strong, but hope is stronger," a statement found in many of Kennon Calahan's books. When I served a congregation where the founding pastor died at the age of 44 after serving for 14 years, this phrase was one of the things we held onto as we worked together through the grief and moved the mission and ministry of the congregation forward.

What is God's preferred future for our lives, our congregations, our synods, and the ELCA? Pat Keifert, systematician at Luther Seminary in St. Paul, Minnesota, asks a similar question about congregations in his lectures. I invite you to pray, talk about, debate, and wrestle with this question. God's Spirit is up to something! The number-one priority for ELCA synods during planning conversations in 2002 was evangelical witness (Kenneth W. Inskeep and Kendra Monroe, "Churchwide Planning Process: Synod Strategic Planning Session Summary Report," ELCA Department for Research and Evaluation, September 12, 2002).

> *In the days to come, as God calls us into this new future, we will have our growing pains, too.*

A new evangelism strategy, passed by the 2003 ELCA churchwide assembly, calls the church to pray, develop faithful and fruitful leadership, grow gracious disciples, and start and renew congregations. (To see the entire strategy, "Sharing Faith in a New Century: A Vision for Evangelism in the Evangelical Lutheran Church in America," visit www.elca.org/visionevangelism/EvangelismStrategyFinal.pdf.) God has been inspiring us to take baby steps. We are learning how to take bigger steps as we live in and live out the good news that has marked us and claimed us forever.

But this will mean change. And change is hard.

Between seventh and eighth grade, for example, I grew six inches taller. I was excited about this because I wanted to play professional football. I went from being a short guy to being one of the tallest guys in my class. I also became incredibly uncoordinated and clumsy while I got used to my body. The worst part was laying in bed with growing pains. My bones were growing so fast that my tendons could not keep up.

In the days to come, as God calls us into this new future, we will have our growing pains, too. We will not always move smoothly. We will stumble at times. Parts of the church will grow into Christ's future faster than others. We will be stretched as Christians, congregations, synods, and the ELCA. Instead of becoming fearful and retreating, I hope we will celebrate and rejoice in what God is up to now.

The cost of change might be enough to stop us, if we did not follow a Lord and Savior who went through much more to reach out to us.

We follow our crucified and resurrected Lord into God's future, even though at times we will suffer and feel like we are dying and losing all that we have known (Mark 8:35). Although we want to run away from the pain of change, Christ calls us to lean into the pain. We follow him, trusting in the resurrecting power of God, which has the power to make all things new (2 Corinthians 5:17).

It Is Time to See that We Have Everything We Need

"By God's grace, together we have what we need." That is part of the mission statement for the Southwestern Minnesota Synod. It is true for all of us as we follow our Lord. This book's purpose is not to give you another chapter in your "book of should." Instead, we have invited you to see what God is up to in our midst and to imagine where God is calling us in the days to come. Our risk-taking Lord has a mission and ministry for each and every baptized one. As we hear the good news, not only are we given the gift of forgiveness and new life, but we also are given the amazing call to share the good news with all people. I don't have it all figured out. Nobody does. But by God's grace, together, we have everything we need to start the journey.

Claimed and Inviting

We have an inviting God. Our God does not invite only the good, smart, powerful, rich, or cool people, like the popular host of a junior high party. Instead, God sent Jesus to invite the broken, poor, socially outcast, sick, and the least likely. Christ Jesus and the God who sent him claim and invite us even though we are all messed up.

I am far from a perfect Christian, father, husband, child, or pastor. All of us know that our lives, our congregations, and our pastors are far from perfect. I know that as a new bishop, I am far from perfect. Yet our gracious God finds ways to use our imperfect witness to do God's work. In fact, in history, it seems that God takes joy in using messed up, confused, and lost people to do God's work. No matter how messed up you are, God is inviting you to join the party of God's kingdom and community that gathers in the shadow of the cross of Christ.

"I have not been in a church for 25 years before tonight." Pat came up to me at a wedding. She pointed across the room and said her friend Judy told her she had to come and talk to me. That night began a three-year journey in which Judy would invite and bring her friend to worship. In our conversations through the years, Pat shared the anxiety she felt in entering the church for the first time on a Sunday morning. She shared her questions. She began a journey of reading, thinking, and growing. God was up to something. I got to be a witness to God's work and Pat's. God used many other people as witnesses, too. God's Spirit was inviting Pat back into her journey of a growing faith life. Now if you look for her you usually find her beside a friend she has invited to worship. God is not done with her, her friend, me, or you.

> *Engaging evangelism is more of a process than an event.*

All of us continue to need to be evangelized, to hear the gift of the good news. The gift also calls us to grow deeper into the life of our crucified and resurrected Lord. Engaging evangelism is more of a process than an event. It is a daily return to the waters of our baptism. God knows that those inside and outside the body of Christ continue to need an ongoing evangelical witness to the good news. We know God's love best in Jesus' life, death, and resurrection. Meeting Jesus changes us, sets us free, and gives us hope.

Yet, we worry about talking about our faith. We are afraid we will say the wrong things. We have witnessed "the practices of evangelists become un-evangelical—that is, manipulative, legalistic, etc.—when the service of delivering the message across a relationship is replaced by attempts to make others join an organization, practice a piety or identify with an ideology and thereby become moral or 'spiritual' " (Marcus Kunz, "The Work of Evangelists" presentation at First Call Theological Education event, February 8, 1999). Our fears often freeze us into a different sin—we don't say anything. We fail to love and serve our neighbor by being an evangelical witness.

We all need to find places and ways to develop our vocabulary, grammar of faith, and "gospel fluency," which is characterized by message delivery that is true to Christ's good work, happens at the right time . . . and happens in the language of the audience or people (Marcus Kunz, "The Work of Evangelists"). When I finished the seminary after deeply drinking of my favorite theologians, I could hardly talk about my faith without making people's eyes glaze over. They thought I was speaking in tongues. Fortunately, I was invited to teach a class on evangelism. As I taught this class, I learned to be more comfortable and competent in listening to other people's spiritual stories, sharing my own story, and celebrating God's story. We practiced skills and waited for opportunities to witness in the days until the next class. The point wasn't to scare people into the church, to catch them with our techniques, but rather to grow more comfortable talking about the faith that God had placed inside us through the work of God's Spirit.

God is inviting us to reach out to all people with the story of Jesus. This is God's central mission! And the good news is for all generations. We have to love our children and our grandchildren enough to listen to them. In hearing their questions, hopes, and longings, God will surprise us. We will be blessed as we grow deeper in faith and love through their questions and witness. Because we love our neighbors as we have been loved, we will at times need to adjust or give up things we have loved and appreciated. In the sacrifice, we will be surprised by God with blessings we have not imagined. As God uses us to do the missionary work of translating the good news into the cultures and contexts God has placed us in, we will have the joy of watching what happens when people hear and grow deeper in the sweet mystery of God's grace (ourselves included).

God invites us to share the good news with people of all cultures. Jesus loved people and proclaimed the good news of God's kingdom to people of many cultures, but particularly to those who were seen as untouchable and unclean. God's Spirit calls us to invite people who are different from us. Jesus calls us to reach out to left-wingers and right-wingers, blue collars and white collars, rural people and city people, rich and poor, young and old, straight people and gay people, high-culture people and hard-living people, sinners of every shape and size.

God's Spirit wants to invite them into Jesus. God invites them into a community that gathers around our crucified and resurrected Lord in awe, repentance, wonder, and joy. Because of God's grace that claims and equips us, we can invite and welcome all kinds of people to learn more about what it means to follow Jesus.

To reach our culture, congregations may need to learn more about *celebrating* the good news. Instead of being God-talk police, we need to give people space, support, and encouragement so that they can learn how to speak about their faith. Instead of controlling people through and hiding behind our great theology, we need to encourage people to grow more comfortable speaking about their spiritual lives.

_____

God invites us to prune anything that blocks our evangelical witness.

_____

In our previous home, we had two big apple trees in our backyard. They did not produce many apples, so I finally asked someone for help and guidance. He told me that I had to prune the trees to help them flower more and produce more fruit. That seemed odd to me. So I followed his instructions only on one tree. On the other I did not do it. As the summer unfolded, one tree was covered with flowers and twice as many apples. I smiled at my lack of faith in my guide.

In order for our evangelical witness to bear fruit, I suspect we will need to do some pruning, too. We might be overly cautious and under-prune. Which branches need to be removed? Our current pattern of inviting people once every 21, 25, or 28 years to join us at worship would be one good branch to remove. We will have to prune away our assumption that everyone automatically knows what we are doing and why. Finally, we will need to prune away our tendency to argue and fight. As Ruben Duran from the ELCA churchwide staff has said, "The harvest is plentiful and the workers are arguing" (Global mission event, Southwestern Minnesota Synod, February, 2003).

God invites us to prune anything that blocks our evangelical witness. In the process we will make space for new growth. When we prune away "country club mentality," we will have more room to grow disciples, followers, and apprentices of Jesus. When we prune away the branches that block our urgent task of inviting people deeper in faith, we will be surprised by how God opens doors for the sharing of our faith. When we prune away the fear that keeps us from welcoming everyone, especially the hard-living people of our time (who incidentally look a lot like the folks Jesus spent most of his time reaching out to in his ministry) we will be amazed at the gifts and blessings they bring to share with us.

Instead of giving up on us, God continues to invite, lure, call, and send us. This is sheer grace. Through Jesus we know that God loves us in spite of our messed up lives. Our resurrecting God has something in mind for us. Christ Jesus invites us to follow him and trust more deeply still in the undeserved love, presence, and power of our God.

Equipped and Equipping

We have an equipping Lord and God. Jesus invited a small group of apprentices to follow and learn from him. He equipped them to be sent. If Jesus did not do all of the ministry, but rather trained and equipped his followers, how did we get stuck in the game of "pastor fetch" in our understanding of how to do church? You know the game. Someone has an idea or sees something happening in another church, then says, "Pastor, you go do it." We would do better to ask, "How could we train or apprentice all the baptized to share and do the ministry?"

I had a conversion experience in my previous call. The congregation had two full-time pastors but, because of financial problems, went to one full-time pastor and a half-time interim pastor. We decided to train, equip, and use part-time staff and our lay leadership in more aggressive ways than I had ever imagined. I became more of a coach than a player in all the ministries. I put a sign up on my door that said, "The Equipment Room," based on an idea another pastor, Lou Forney, had shared with me. People would stop, laugh, and tease me about the sign. But every time I walked into my office I remembered that my primary mission was to "equip the saints" (Ephesians 4:12). What we found was that the congregation's ministry actually grew in health, vitality, and size. I felt less overworked and overwhelmed. I grew more and more fond of saying, "Thank God the ministers are here" as I would find people caring, serving, listening, and loving.

Congregations, synods, and the ELCA exist to grow *apprentices of Jesus,* not church members. Watch what happens when you focus on equipping people to engage in the ministry they were called to in their baptism. Some ways to equip people are found in our heritage. We need to remember what Luther knew when he created the Small Catechism— the primary place where the faith is caught and taught is in the home (by families of all shapes). Other tools for equipping people are faith practices, called "God-shaped and God shaping activities" by Martha E. Stortz ("Faith Practices, Faith Lives: A Lutheran Perspective on Faith Practices," Teach the Faith Initiative, *Congregation Planning Guide*). Seven faith practices were included in the Teach the Faith Initiative, an ELCA-wide Call to Discipleship adopted in 1997: prayer, inviting, giving, studying, encouraging, worshiping, and serving. There are many other faith practices worth celebrating as well. Faith practices serve the church by equipping and shaping the lives of Christians. They are like my braces that slowly, steadily reshaped my mouth and smile over the course of years. The practices are not the giver of graces, but they are some of God's gifts.

When we focus on equipping people for evangelical witness, leadership preparation looks different. The preparation of coaches who lead God's local team of people making ministry and mission happen will look different from preparing congregational chaplains. We will need to encourage people with different personalities, gifts, skills, and experiences to be public servants of the gospel. These people will speak in fresh voices about the truth we know in Christ Jesus. They will articulate the faith in a public way for a culture whose roots in the Christian tradition are thinning. With courage, these leaders will continue to confront sin and bring the good news of God's forgiving grace. They will be able to see, encourage, train, and call forth the assets people and congregations have. They will actively train, develop, and mobilize the gifts of lay people (paid, compensated volunteers, and volunteer ministers). They will be evangelical witnesses who take their role seriously, but take God more seriously still.

Sent and Sending

We have a sending Lord and God who believes more in us than we at times believe in ourselves. Not only have I come to reclaim the old and good word *disciple*, but I also love the word *apostle*, which literally means "sent one." Both of those words not only describe people in Jesus' time, but also people in our time. We are disciples (learners) so that we can be apostles. As we serve as apostles, we cannot help but come back to sit at the feet of our Master.

Where to next? God sends us to live out our many different vocations or callings in and for God's world. I have been called to be a child of God, a child, a spouse, a parent, a neighbor, a friend, a citizen, and so on. God sends us into the common ordinary work of life where we care for our neighbors and this creation. You are an apostle—a witness in your everyday life. Witnessing is not a project or program. We are witnesses as Christians, churches, synods, and a denomination. God has, can, and will use us in ways we understand and in other ways beyond our imagination. It happens every day.

You are always sharing your faith.

If you are not sure where God is sending you, then listen to the assets that God has given you. When you listen to your gifts, you catch strong hints about where God is sending you. This is God's *"Great Permission"* that sets you free to love your neighbor, celebrate your life, and dance in all the challenging defeats and opportunities of life (Bob Sitze, *The Great Permission: An Asset-Based Field Guide for Congregations*, Evangelical Lutheran Church in America, 2002). Jesus says to you and me, "You will be my witnesses in Jerusalem, in all Judea and Samaria, and to the ends of the earth" (Acts 1:8). This is not an imperative . . . something we have to do. This is a statement of fact. You are always sharing your faith. We all need evangelizing and God uses us to evangelize. Remember the promise at the end of the Great Commission: "I am with you always" (Matthew 28:20). You are never alone.

Summary

A few years back I went to a huge water slide park for the first time in a decade. We stood in line to go down the biggest and newest slide right away, because we knew the lines would get longer as the day went by. The higher we got, the more foolish our idea seemed to me. Finally we were at the very top. The teenage lifeguard was motioning for me to get into the water and go down the steep tube. All of a sudden, I was not sure I wanted to do it. I was scared. I don't know why. I guess I knew I would be out of control. And it had been years since I had been on a big water slide. The lifeguard looked at me and said, "Come on . . . let's go." And I jumped in the cold water and started my journey. At first I was screaming . . . scared . . . fighting being out of control . . . flipping, turning suddenly . . . and then I remembered that I was safe in a tube . . . and my screams of fear turned to screams of joy.

Our Lord Jesus is calling "come and follow." So what are we waiting for? Let's go!

As God calls us to slide in the channels of grace into God's future, our fears and anxieties slip away as we remember that we can float in God's grace and trust in the channels of our God's love. In the meantime, maybe we could start by screaming . . . AMEN!!! At first in fear . . . then in hope . . . and finally in joy.

Our Lord Jesus is calling us to "come and follow." So what are we waiting for? Let's go!

For Reflection and Discussion

1. Be honest: What has your congregation been focusing on? What does it need to be focusing on in order to be a part of God's mission where you live? In other words, what does it mean for you — and your congregation — to be faithful and fruitful followers of Jesus *now*?

2. You have everything you need, starting with this fact: God claims you, through Jesus Christ. God is inviting YOU to follow! When was the last time you really heard this invitation loud and clear? Where has our gracious God been inviting you to lately?

3. In the last year, how often have you invited someone to simply join you in worship? Who do you know who needs an invitation today?

4. What would you do to grow pastors and other public servants who could equip the saints to do ministry in their daily vocations? How are you being called to look at YOUR ministry differently?

5. God is sending us out! What does this mean for you? Are you scared? Excited? Both? What will you do NEXT, after reading this book? Make a list. And pray, pray, pray for God's help and guidance to carry it out!

Recommended Resources

Arias, Mortimer, and Alan Johnson. *The Great Commissions: Biblical Models for Evangelism.* Nashville: Abingdon Press, 1992.

Bass, Dorothy, ed. *Practicing Our Faith: A Way of Life for a Searching People.* San Francisco: Jossey-Bass, 1998.

Bowen, John P. *Evangelism for "Normal" People: Good News for Those Looking for a Fresh Approach.* Minneapolis: Augsburg Fortress, 2002.

Foss, Michael W. *Power Surge: Six Marks of Discipleship for a Changing Church.* Minneapolis: Fortress Press, 2000.

Fryer, Kelly A., and Timothy J. Ressmeyer. *Dancing Down the Hallway: Spiritual Reflections for Every Day.* Minneapolis: Augsburg Fortress, 2001.

Fryer, Kelly A. *No Experience Necessary: On-the-Job Training for the Life of Faith.* Minneapolis: Augsburg Fortress, 1999.

_____. *Reclaiming the "L" Word: Renewing the Church from Its Lutheran Core.* Minneapolis: Augsburg Fortress, 2003.

Hagen, Andy, and Rahel Hahn. *A Joyful Harvest: A Program of "Welcome" Evangelism.* Minneapolis: Augsburg Fortress, 2003.

Jesús, Miguel de. *Beyond Our Comfort Zone: Developing Social Ministry Programs in Multiethnic Settings.* Minneapolis: Augsburg Fortress, 2002.

Jones, Tony. *Postmodern Youth Ministry.* Grand Rapids, Michigan: Zondervan, 2001.

Kallestad, Walt. *Turn Your Church Inside Out: Building a Community for Others.* Minneapolis: Augsburg Fortress, 2001.

Keifert, Patrick R. *Welcoming the Stranger: A Public Theology of Worship and Evangelism.* Minneapolis: Fortress Press, 1994.

Klaiber, Walter. *Call and Response: Biblical Foundations of a Theology of Evangelism.* Nashville: Abingdon Press, 1997.

Kolb, Robert, and Timothy J. Wengert, eds. *The Book of Concord: The Confessions of the Evangelical Lutheran Church.* Minneapolis: Fortress Press, 2000.

Luther, Martin. *On Christian Liberty.* Minneapolis: Fortress Press, 2003.

McLaren, Brian D. *A New Kind of Christian: A Tale of Two Friends on a Spiritual Journey.* San Francisco: Jossey-Bass, 2001.

————. *The Church on the Other Side: Doing Ministry in the Postmodern Matrix.* Grand Rapids, Michigan: Zondervan, 2003.

Nessan, Craig L. *Beyond Maintenance to Mission: A Theology of the Congregation.* Minneapolis: Augsburg Fortress, 1999.

Nissen, Johannes. *New Testament and Mission: Historical and Hermeneutical Perspectives.* Frankfurt, Germany: Peter Lang, 1999.

Poling-Goldenne, David, and L. Shannon Jung. *Discovering Hope: Building Vitality in Rural Congregations.* Minneapolis: Augsburg Fortress, 2001.

Smith, Chuck, Jr. *The End of the World . . . As We Know It: Clear Direction for Bold and Innovative Ministry in a Postmodern World.* Colorado Springs, Colorado: WaterBrook Press, 2001.

Van Dunk, Greg. *Let the Glory of the Lord Rise Among Us: Growing a Church in the Heart of the City.* Minneapolis: Augsburg Fortress, 2002.

Vieth, Gene Edward, Jr. *Postmodern Times: A Christian Guide to Contemporary Thought and Culture.* Crossway Books, 1994.

Web sites

ELCA Department for Research and Evaluation:
www.elca.org/re

ELCA Evangelism Strategy:
www.elca.org/dcm/evangelism

Emerging Church:
www.emergingchurch.org